Grounded
in God

Best wishes for faith,
many more years of
hope, love & laughter.
Deacon Jim & Ann Cave

Grounded in God

A Mature Experience of Faith

Jim Cavera and Ann Cavera

Liguori
LIGUORI, MISSOURI

Imprimi Potest:
Thomas D. Picton, C.Ss.R.
Provincial, Denver Province
The Redemptorists

Published by Liguori Publications
Liguori, Missouri
www.liguori.org

Library of Congress Cataloging-in-Publication Data

Cavera, Jim.
    Grounded in God : a mature experience of faith / Jim Cavera and Ann Cavera.—1st. ed.
      p. cm.
    Includes bibliographical references.
    ISBN 0-7648-1408-7
    1. Christian life—Catholic authors. 2. Christian life—Meditations. 3. Aging—Religious aspects—Catholic Church. I. Cavera, Ann. II. Title.
BX2350.3.C39 2006
242'.3—dc22
                                          2006002069

Liguori Publications, a nonprofit corporation, is an apostolate of the Redemptorists. To learn more about the Redemptorists, visit *Redemptorists.com.*

Printed in the United States of America
10 09 08 07 06   5 4 3 2 1
First edition

Dedication

*To Cate and Rachel for giving us new life
and for keeping our hearts young.*

Contents

3. Lent

4. Holy Week/Triduum

5. Easter

Introduction

We cannot pick up a magazine or newspaper without reading about people over the age of fifty who are out having remarkable adventures. Elderly women are winning marathons and climbing mountains. Aging men are flying off in hot air balloons and sailing around the world...alone. A few years ago, even John Glenn got himself shot back into space. For the most part, we wish all of them would stop. We don't begrudge any of them their late-life adventures. It is just that they keep setting up unrealistic standards for the rest of us who are not going anywhere anytime soon—that is, we're not planning trips to space or to exotic, distant retreats. Instead of creating fantastic adventures, we prefer to use this time in our lives to sink our roots deeper in faith. Being grounded in God keeps our sight on the ultimate adventure, which is life wherever we find ourselves. Instead of focusing on the end of life, we intend to focus on living life to the end.

While we may not have sailed around the world, we did set off for St. Louis last spring just to see the sights. Like thousands of other tourists, we settled ourselves into a small, enclosed car to ride up through the steel curve to the top of the Gateway Arch. On the way up, we felt our little car frequently shift slightly as it made adjustments for the curve. If the car had failed to make any of the frequent adjustments necessary along the way, we would have been stuck. So it is with us. Adjusting along the way becomes part of aging well. How do we do it? What about our aging bodies and minds?

In the past twenty years, a lot of research has been done on the aging process. So far, only one predictable factor has been determined: reaction time does decrease with age. Even though the details of how we will age cannot be predicted, we can do our best to keep fit in spirit, mind, and body. While we may not have complete control over the aging process, we still make choices each day that affect our spiritual, mental, and physical health. Making wise choices in these areas helps us to live Christian lives focused on the needs of others instead of ourselves.

So what should be our attitude toward life as we age? Let others our age fly off in balloons if they like. This book is about choosing to seize the day by making the most of what we have in our adult lives. Time takes on a different meaning as we age. The simple joy in everyday love and laughter is all the sweeter because we are aware of the preciousness of those moments. The miseries some of us face are bearable only because we know from experience how each stage of life is temporary.

Together we will explore the love, laughter, and pain that cycle through our mature lives. Like our journey through the church year, these narratives are organized around the liturgical calendar—from the expectation of Advent to the joy of Christmas; from the reflection of Lent to the pain of the crucifixion; from the exaltation of the resurrection to the road to Emmaus; and from the insight of Ordinary Time toward the assuring promise that Christ is with us through it all. Whether read from front to back, or starting in the middle and jumping around, the stories invite you to find your own place in God's goodness. Here, the liturgical seasons free you to jump in wherever you like—to find God in your particular place and experience.

In Luke 20:38, Jesus says that God is God not of the dead, but of the living, for to him all are in fact alive. Part of the joy of living in faith is the understanding that as we age—even as we near and pass through death—there is only life in God's creation. "Grounded in God" means taking each day with acceptance and gratitude. Through ever-deepening faith, every day becomes an adventure.

1
Advent

*Therefore, keep awake—for you do not know when the
master of the house will come, in the evening, or at midnight, or at cockcrow, or at dawn, or else he may find
you asleep when he comes suddenly.*

MARK 13:35–36

The Ideal Family

Thanksgiving, Advent, and Christmas are all about families.
We think of festive meals, decorating the house, and the
gathering of brothers, sisters, aunts, uncles, and cousins—all
wrapped in a spirit of peace and goodwill. If an ideal family could
be found, surely it could be found in Scripture.

By checking out a few of the families in the Bible, we made a
number of interesting discoveries. Jealousy drove a wedge between the first two brothers; the result was murder. Everybody
considered Noah to be a lunatic; his wife put up with him any-
way. Sarah followed Abraham from one country to another before his heart finally told him he was home. Isaac and Rebecca
had a son named Jacob who lied to his father and cheated his
brother. What's worse, his mother helped him. Jacob had twelve
sons by four different women. Neither the women nor the sons

could get along. The older boys hated their little brother Joseph so much they sold him into slavery. King David had a house full of sons. When David's son Amnon violated his own half sister Tamar, her brother Absalom killed Amnon. Absalom plotted to take over the throne and ran his father out of town. Even when David was on his deathbed, there was no peace in his house. Families in the New Testament had no better luck. The marriage of Mary and Joseph began in unusual circumstances. Their baby was born away from home in less than ideal surroundings. The Holy Family had to spend years hiding in a foreign country. Later, Jesus' cousin John, the only child of wearied Zechariah and Elizabeth, was beheaded because he said things that made people in high places uncomfortable. No matter how hard we searched, every family mentioned seemed to have its own share of trouble.

Is it any wonder when we look around today that it is difficult to find an ideal family? Nobody wants to invite Uncle John to family gatherings because he always drinks too much. Cousin Edna never did learn when to stop talking. Can't we leave her at the nursing home this year? One friend says that she has a daughter-in-law who won't speak to her. The grown children of another friend get together for the holidays without her because they don't like her new husband. Two brothers won't speak because of a business deal that soured five years ago. And you know what Martha did to Betty just two days before her wedding? Although it was thirty years ago, they still won't sit together in the same room. Because we can't invite them together, we won't ask either of them.

When it comes to families in Scripture, God included those guilty of strange behavior, cheats, scoundrels, and criminals. While some of those families were highly dysfunctional, even by today's standards, God used them as instruments in his plan of salvation.

When you look at your own strange family, whom are you not including this year? When God's presence lives in us, no one gets left out.

John the Baptist

Have you ever wondered what people saw in John the Baptist? Was it mere curiosity that caused them to leave the comfort of their homes and travel to the outskirts of civilization to hear him? Perhaps. After all, John dressed in rough clothes, ate honey and grasshoppers, preferred the desolation of the desert, and, above all, said things no one else dared to say against established religious leaders. We believe we would have been curious enough to go and check him out…at least once. John was more than a mere object of curiosity. In a strong voice that echoed against the rocks, he displayed such boldness one quickly forgot about his disheveled appearance. People found themselves drawn to his voice and to a message that confronted and challenged them. Though harsh at times, his words did not drive people away. Scripture describes large crowds coming to hear John, implying that people returned time and again and brought friends with them.

In our community, we have a certain television commercial where a man shouts at the top of his voice about all the "bargains" available in his furniture showroom. We are bombarded with descriptions of tables, chairs, sofas, sectionals, and mattresses all at never-before-seen, unbelievably low prices. The man appears to spew out words without ever taking a breath. Our automatic response is to reach for the mute button on the remote control, which once was described by Ann's father as the greatest invention since television. In less than a second, we find ourselves removed from the annoying babble. People did not turn John off. He drew them in to the point where they asked his advice about what they were to do. His message, both direct and simple, challenged them to share what little they had, to treat one another honestly and justly, to repent, and to come to the water to be baptized.

John's appearance on the scene some two thousand years ago had a disturbing effect. He called for change not in a policy or in a system, but in the minds and hearts of each individual. He gave the people hope by speaking of the one who would come after him and about the need to prepare for salvation. Those in power saw John and his message as a threat to their ways, a threat which has continued through the centuries.

Today, there are many who urge us to focus only on our worldly concerns and to "mute out" John's prophetic call for repentance and a change of heart. Understandably, it is hard to hear John's words against the din that surrounds us, the frantic pace of the season, and our often self-imposed overwhelming schedules. Advent calls us to a time of personal renewal and quiet anticipation.

Expecting the Unexpected

Years ago we discovered it is just as easy to make two pans of lasagna as it is to make one. So, on the first Monday of Advent, while making a pan of lasagna to serve the children during the holidays, I (Ann) filled an extra pan. Both went into the freezer downstairs. Around 2 PM that same day, my mother's cousin Callie called and announced that she and her husband were sitting in a local restaurant out on the highway. How strange, I thought. Cousin Callie is a sensible woman in her early seventies. She lives some eight hundred miles away in Florida. I wondered how she could be here with her husband because poor Rufus had died a year earlier! As things turned out, Callie had gotten herself a new husband. They had eloped the week before—immediately after their grown children had started making far more elaborate wedding plans than either of them wanted. After a simple, private wedding, they set off touring the country, surprising unsuspecting relatives along the way.

Of course we were glad to see them. I found myself inviting them to come for a lasagna supper. With a quick dash downstairs, I resurrected the spare pan before it had a chance to freeze. That evening we enjoyed two friendships, one old and the other new. Callie's new husband Ray, a retired Marine, had a great sense of humor, and he and Callie obviously shared a deep love for each other.

Callie and Ray opened the door to Advent for us with a reminder that Advent is not just about waiting. Rather, it is about being prepared for the unexpected. If we have an extra loaf of bread to share, an extra blanket to give, an extra box of cards to send, or even an extra pan of lasagna, we can wait with hope and allow God to decide how to send Christ into our lives.

As for us, this Advent season began, not with the arrival of our children, but with the sparkle in Callie's eyes. As for Ray? He has a heart full of kindness and laughter. And, he loves lasagna.

Plate Spinning

The late 1950s found us watching the *Ed Sullivan Show* on Sunday nights. One of our favorite acts was a man who knew how to spin plates on top of thin rods. By frantically running back and forth, he managed to keep more than a dozen plates spinning all at once. The suspense mounted as plates wobbled, then tilted, only to be kept from crashing by a last-second tap.

Lately, we feel like plate spinners. This thought came home after a friend asked me to pass some information on to Jim when

I saw him at supper. Then I remembered that our plans were for me to buy a fast-food supper for Jim and pick him up after work. He would eat his supper in the car while I drove us home. There, I would hop out of the car and he would drive on to teach his night class. Now, presumably, I needed to drive and share information while he gobbled down his hamburger—adding even another dimension to our "supper hour." Plate spinning. We are all spinning plates as we try to keep up with our ever-expanding calendars.

Years ago in a book entitled *Future Shock*, Alvin Toffler described how change can come about so rapidly that it leaves people in a state of shock. With such a time upon us, we find ourselves overwhelmed with change, much of which has to do with communication. From personal computers that fit in the palm of the hand to powerful digital phones that offer us instant connection to the world, we find ourselves immersed in products designed to keep us in touch and save time. Where is all this time we have supposedly saved? It is lost, we discover, in still another round of plate spinning. We are as happy as the next person when our computer tells us we have new e-mail. We are also sometimes let down by two- or three-sentence e-mail masquerading. Sometimes we feel as though a friend has given us just a quick tap to keep the friendship spinning. We long for more substance in our relationships.

I am old enough to remember sitting beside my mother and aunts while we all shelled peas. Under the cover of work, more real conversation took place than in any psychotherapy session. Over the past several years, a friend and I have taken occasional walks. The official business is the exercise. The unofficial, but far more important, agenda is the unloading of our minds and hearts while we walk. When we make space for communication in the course of our work, the ministry of friendship happens.

We have come upon a season meant to slow us down long enough to be able to spend time with relatives, listen to a child, or write a letter to a friend. Even washing the dishes after a holiday meal once provided a chance to catch up on the family news. Perhaps this season we can make time for the inefficiency of real conversation. To do otherwise means we can easily spend the Advent season doing nothing more than spinning plates.

Waiting in Hope

We have been caught up in memories lately. This is a perfectly legitimate pastime for people in the second half of life in spite of the fact that it is not always appreciated by our children. This latest wave of nostalgia came about when our college-age daughter borrowed some old slides from our Peace Corps days in West Africa for her student-teaching project.

Those pictures took us back some thirty-eight years. We could still remember the names of some of our African friends pictured there with us. The pictures captured the fact that we were very happy. We looked pretty good for a couple of twenty-three-year-olds just out of college and thousands of miles from home.

What the pictures did not show was that we were pretty much clueless about many things in life. Our parents realized this and kept us surrounded with daily prayer. We survived our Peace Corps days and grew stronger in many ways. Both of us had come from solid faith backgrounds. We were well-grounded in our Christianity, but, like many young adults, we felt in control of our lives. We had not yet encountered the reality of our stupidity, helplessness, and vulnerability. Although we tried to move forward with confidence, we often drifted, letting the flow of circumstances carry us along. Thankfully, our parents continued to pray for us. Somewhere along the way, we became aware of the hard realities of the adult world. We rediscovered our faith, which had been there all along. It didn't hit us like a bolt of lightning, but it sank in gradually over time.

In marriage preparation sessions, we have often told couples that the grace of the sacrament unfolds later when you discover that the person you are with is not the person you expected. In spite of that, a deeper love takes root and later blooms. Perhaps we could use this same example with the grace of the sacraments of initiation. With a little effort, we can recall being confirmed in our faith through the power of the Holy Spirit in our teen years. As young adults, we may have given little thought to the grace of those sacraments. Yet, maybe the grace of baptism and confirmation led to the blossoming of a deeper, more mature faith and infused us with both insight and humility years later.

Today we join with other parents in praying for our children to rediscover Jesus Christ in their lives and embrace their faith anew. The groundwork was laid years ago and now we wait "in joyful hope for the coming of our savior Jesus Christ" into the lives of our sons and daughters.

Fair Exchange

It was almost dark when we pulled up to the apartment building south of the city. We didn't know much about the young family we had come to help. The mother, her seven-year-old son, and her six-year-old daughter were starting life over in an empty apartment on a cold December evening. A benefactor had donated beds and a parishioner had loaded everything on his truck. We went along to lend a hand. It did not seem as if the few items we were moving in—beds and bedding, a few lamps, and a couple of child-size beanbag chairs thrown on the truck for good measure—could do much to fill the void of that empty apartment. At least beds meant this little family could sleep warm and off the floor.

The weather had turned cold and damp, signaling the start of true winter. Fall leaves soaked by an earlier rain swirled in the north wind and crept into the entry each time we opened the door. Knowing we would soon be working in the dark, we moved quickly to unload the truck. Hands and elbows banged against door jambs. Strained muscles went unnoticed while we focused completely on the task at hand. Later, our aches and pains reminded us not only of our age but also why we never pursued work in the moving business. For the moment, we focused on assembling metal frames and adjusting them to fit snugly around the box springs. We saved the bulky flexible mattresses until last and then wrestled them up the stairs and around sharp turns.

During this entire venture, the chatter of young voices filled the air. The boy and girl watched closely. As each mattress fell in place, they helped their mother smooth out the linens on the beds. Then, as we headed for the door, the exchange happened. The seven-year-old angel, disguised as a little girl, fished something out of her pocket. She said, "Here, these are for good people" and placed two small seashells into each of our hands. We thanked her, said our goodbyes, and headed for our vehicles in silence. Although none of us said a word at the moment, we all knew we had been paid in full.

That night we were exhausted when we climbed into our own warm bed. We spoke briefly about the day. Both of us had been thinking about the seashells and what they meant to us. The generosity of God surrounds us, and yet how easily we take warm beds, plenty of food, money for utilities, a good coat, a car, and a home for granted. That Advent evening, two seashells placed in the palms of our hands by a child reminded us of our own need for gratitude.

Birds on a Wire

Did you ever notice that when birds sit on a wire they all face in the same direction? Driving early one winter morning, we stopped under a high wire. Thirty or forty birds perched there with feathers fluffed against the cold. The wire swayed a little in the wind.

Two years ago in the week before Advent began, we lost our parish administrator and the "mother" to all of our community. A year ago near the beginning of Advent, Dorothy, our pastor's mother, passed away in the rectory where she had been living with her son. She had been an important member of our community for the past few years, and she remained active in it until her death. Then, for the third year in a row, again at the beginning of Advent, the specter of death stood among us. Sister Darlene, one of our pastoral associates, became so ill following surgery that she ended up on a ventilator in the hospital intensive care unit. She has been part of our community for many years and she is dear to all of us. This third tragedy made us realize that we had had more than enough.

Sister Darlene's peril had a stirring effect on our parish. It was as if a trumpet sounded and our community heard a call to arms. Prayer became our unanimous weapon of choice. The first line of defense became a prayer vigil with two or more people covering every hour around the clock. Many others throughout the diocese and beyond spent time praying frequently for short intervals several times day and night. We kept a spiritual wall around her through which darkness was forbidden to pass. A week later, Sister Darlene became strong enough to be taken off the ventilator, but she still needed much prayer to assist her in her long recovery. A massive wall of prayer held fast until finally, once again, we saw her on a Sunday morning sprinting the distance between the piano in front of the church and the organ in the choir loft. As a parish, we have never been the same since that event. We have rediscovered the ancient power of believers united in heart and purpose through prayer.

Advent is a fitting time of year to remember who we are and the gifts that have been entrusted to us. Of all the gifts God has given us, prayer may be the one most talked about and also the one least used. There is power in prayer that goes far beyond our understanding. It is a way of opening our hearts in a common communion with our Lord. Prayer binds us together as one and connects us directly through the power of the Holy Spirit. Yet, in the middle of this holy season, the specter of war still hangs over our world. Children go hungry in many places including our own towns and cities. When will we have had enough? Too bad it takes such a cold wind to make all of us, like birds on a wire, face in the same direction.

To Be Like a Child

I sat on a bench in the mall while Jim shopped in one of the stores. Our plan was for me to write an Advent column about the first person who sat down and spoke to me. Sounds simple, doesn't it? Unfortunately, the people who sat next to me were stone-faced, silent, crabby, unapproachable grumps. I had almost given up when a screaming child about twenty feet away caught my attention. One tough looking four-year-old boy suddenly had more shopping than he could handle. "No! No! I won't go!" Little fists clenched, arms pumping furiously, he screamed and jumped up and down in a fury. His exhausted mother hardly shot him a backward glance as she walked away and left him standing there in the middle of the mall. The screams got louder and the boy did not budge. After a few seconds, the mother reappeared, grabbed his arm, and pulled him along with her in spite of his protests.

I gave up my plan to get an Advent story from an adult in the mall. Instead, I began focusing on the children. Another mother, eyes glazed, drifted by. Next to her wandered a toddler who had the same dazed look as her mother. The little girl clutched a bag from a bakery. She slowly slid her fingers inside the bag, pulled out a handful of pink frosting, and stuffed it in her mouth. No connection with the coming of Christ here.

Things began to pick up when a blond, pony-tailed girl hurried past with an adult. Both of them carried packages. The girl held up a bag almost as big as she was. She had pulled it up in front of her face so that she viewed the world through the handle of the bag. Maybe all of us need a new way of seeing things.

Just before Jim returned, a curly-haired moppet bounced past. She moved quickly to keep up with her dad, and the hood on the back of her little red coat flopped up and down. Neither parent nor child carried anything at all. As they passed, I heard the sweet, clear sound of the little girl singing. It wasn't a familiar melody, and I couldn't make out the words. The spontaneous song appeared to pour from her heart for no reason other than the joy of singing.

The world around us grows more intense in this holy season. I expected my conversation with a stranger to provide wisdom for Advent. Instead, the answer came unexpectedly from the children. Sometimes I feel like the boy screaming in the mall. Or, my eyes glaze over and I feel trapped in the excess of the season. Other times, loaded with packages, I try to keep up. How much I want to be like the last child, walking through the season encumbered by nothing more than a song from the heart and the joy of Christ filling my soul.

2
Christmas

But Mary treasured all these words and pondered them in her heart.

LUKE 2:19

Shepherds in the Field

Saint Luke's account of the host of angels appearing to the shepherds is one of our favorite parts of the Christmas story. Can you imagine what the shepherds must have felt? Who would believe that the heavens opened, an angel spoke to them, and a host of angels filled the sky with hosannas? This kind of thing just was not supposed to happen, especially to men who were usually given little respect. Many believed that shepherds were no better than thieves because they let their sheep graze on other people's land. What a lonely job, stuck out in the fields with no mail service, no cell phones, and no iPods.® No one came to visit them. They were the last people to hear any news. Yet on one particular night some two thousand years ago, they were the first to hear news so great that it shook the angels from heaven.

That was only the beginning of the story. After the heavenly host disappeared, the shepherds walked to Bethlehem where they found the baby lying in the manger just as they had been told. In the dim light of that stable, they saw joy in the young mother's eyes and pride in the father's stature. They told Mary and Joseph all about the angel's message and the great heavenly host. Then, I imagine, everyone became quiet as they took in the peace of Christ and held it in their hearts.

One of the blessings of marriage is parenthood. Witnessing the birth of a child shakes our souls. Seeing a newborn for the first time fills us with indescribable wonder. When we look into a baby's eyes, we see what Mary and Joseph saw that night: a new beginning filled with possibilities that are limited only by our imagination. If only we could just capture this moment when all of the possibility of heaven comes to earth—if only we could live with this in our hearts every day—what a tremendous difference this would make in our lives and in the lives of those around us.

It is not always easy to be open to the possibility of heaven in this troubled world. We have to work at it. With children we have to see beyond the dirty diapers, the late-night feedings, the toilet training, the childhood illness, and all the other distractions that can dim the light in our hearts. Our lives as parents, in fact our lives as human beings, are constantly filled with distractions that prevent us from seeing the greatness God has in mind for us and the ones we love.

The Christmas celebration reminds us that the infant Jesus brings with him unlimited possibility in our own lives and, through us, to the world as well. At Christmas, the news of Jesus' birth comes to each of us just as it did to those shepherds in the fields. Like them, we are invited to come and see for ourselves that Jesus, our Messiah, is alive and waiting to be discovered. We are urged to look for Jesus not in a particular city as the shepherds did, but rather in the hearts of those we encounter along our life's journey. When we truly see the Christ Child, we will understand that on this night, of all nights, all things are possible.

Christmas Cactus

We all have a mental image of the way Christmas is supposed to be. Christmas happens in a house that is clean and beautifully decorated. A huge pine tree covered with meaningful ornaments we have gathered through the years sparkles in the window. Beautifully wrapped and tagged presents wait beneath the tree. Cards with handwritten notes inside have been sent to friends and family in faraway places. Wonderful aromas pour from the kitchen. Homemade cookies, breads, and pies are ready to be delivered to neighbors and offered to friends who decide to "drop in" on the spur of the moment.

Who do we think makes all this stuff happen? Moms! Legions of tired, overworked moms keep doing their best to turn the image in everybody's head into reality. And what happens when a mom gets too old to lift a spatula? She passes the Christmas mantle on to an unsuspecting daughter or daughter-in-law to keep things going.

Ready or not, Christmas is upon us again. I (Ann) am writing this after a week of scurrying around without actually completing much of anything. Our artificial tree is up in one corner. It is graced by lights and a few lonely candy canes. None of us has had time to hang the ornaments. Cards still need to be sent. Presents are both bought and un-bought, wrapped and waiting to be wrapped. Ingredients for cookies are in the cupboard...if only we had time to mix them.

I can hear the men out there saying, "Mothers should delegate." That is true. Many women do have men in their lives happy to pitch in if asked. But you see, Christmas is a "woman thing." Always has been. It must have begun with Mary arranging hay in the manger around the baby Jesus. Because of her one magnificent, forever *fiat* ("Let it be done unto me"), a stable became the birthplace for a king and multitudes of moms are still trying to arrange the hay in the manger.

Our daughter Katie and her husband, Woody, flew in from California recently to spend the holidays with us. We were grateful they were only an hour late. So many flights had been canceled due to bad weather. They arrived happy to be home, even though not a single piece of their luggage arrived with them. By this morning, two of their three bags had turned up. They fly often and did not seem to be the least bit disturbed by any of this.

In spite of late flights, terrible weather, lost luggage and unfinished Christmas agendas, we found a beautiful, unexpected gift in a corner of the basement. This is our first Christmas without Grandma Smith. Her Christmas cactus is still on our basement windowsill, just where she left it. This cactus has not bloomed in years. We discovered it full of buds promising to open by Christmas day. It is as though Grandma is letting us know that she is still present in our lives. In the middle of so much unfinished business, Grandma's cactus reminds us that the miracle of Christmas enters our lives not through our busy preparations, but through our simply being open to it.

Secrets in Closets

At Christmastime, tons of gifts are hidden in closets. In fact, in this land of overabundance, many of us also have gifts stored in attics, trunks, and even under the bed. Before my brother and I (Ann) were twelve, we knew about the closet where our parents hid our Christmas toys. Only once did we peek at those gifts ahead of time. Once was enough for us to realize, even at that young age, that gifts taken before they are given lose their luster. Secrets locked in closets need to be honored.

Still, we can't help but wonder what gifts God has in store for us. These secrets will all be revealed in God's own good time. Although in this world we can never fully comprehend God or the mystery of his plans, we do know that our God of grace reveals himself through his gifts, which often come as surprises. For instance, the Israelites knew their savior would appear, but who would have expected the gift of the victorious Messiah to come as a vulnerable baby wrapped in swaddling clothes?

God often sends gifts disguised as people into our lives. They overtake us with their secrets stored in closets, just like at Christmas. Some arrive when we most need them and when we least expect them. We are surprised by the joy and richness of new love and friendship. Others come in plain wrappers and we do not take time to open them. Like the Israelites who missed the messiah, we let some go unrecognized as the magnificent gifts God intended them to be. For instance, how can we who own Christ still allow a world of countless children to sleep cold, hungry, and alone?

Recently, a young mother told us that for strength during the most difficult hours of labor for the birth of her son, she held fast to an image of her pastor holding up the Eucharist at the consecration. What a mighty image to accompany the birth of a child. Perhaps if we had keener ears, we could hear the angels sing at the birth of every child. In this season, we stack our prayers as deep as snow with heaven touching earth. Our prayer this year is that we might have our eyes opened to recognize God's promise of salvation renewed to us in the birth of each newborn child.

Family Recipes

One of our family Christmas treasures is clipped to the side of the refrigerator. In 1976, we cut out a recipe for cinnamon pecan rolls from the back of a sack of flour. Now, greasy, stiff, and splattered, the recipe on this scrap of paper has become a vital part of our Christmas morning. It takes four hours to create three pans of these warm, sticky rolls and to fill the house with the aroma of hot bread and cinnamon. We make these on Christmas Eve and any other time a grown child is able to come home. Even as we write this, a batch of dough will soon be rising in the oven.

Our family has other recipes, and I am sure yours does too. When we open the back door to Grandpa Cavera's house after a nine-hour drive to Grand Rapids, warm air rushes out along with the smell of spaghetti sauce. We know that the ingredients have come from a local, family-owned Italian store. This sauce will have been simmering for as long as we have been traveling. It is an incredibly thick, rich, wine-laden sauce full of meatballs and chunks of homemade Italian sausage. Even if you could buy sauce like this, you could not buy the love that created it. On the other side of the family, the very sight of Grandma Smith's large clay pot from the early 1940s reminds us of Sundays and coming home from church to lift it from the oven where a roast, potatoes, and carrots had simmered to perfection for our family dinner.

Family recipes bind us together and call us home. The older we become, the more we appreciate the gift of family and the fundamental things that hold us together. Family recipes are among our basic memories and serve as invisible signatures in our minds and hearts. They are treasured and honored, uniting one generation to the next. If you know the taste of Grandma's pot roast, you have eaten at her table. If you can call to mind Grandpa's spaghetti sauce, you are a Cavera.

Even as our appreciation of family deepens, so does our appreciation of the Eucharist and what it means to be brothers and sisters in Christ. Years ago, we heard someone say that no food is as thoroughly destroyed as grain and grape before they can become bread and wine. Christ's choice of something so crushed and broken for our spiritual family meal calls to mind not only his gift to us, but the gifts of our brothers and sisters who have been crushed and broken for our faith. In every language, the central act of our faith calls us and binds us as family. When we receive the Eucharist, we accept divine love that makes the Eucharist possible. In this most wondrous of all meals, we know Christ…and together we are family.

Peaceful Intentions

One of the first cards we received before Christmas came from a young friend who married this past summer. "I feel so silly sending you a 'thank-you note' for a blender that you didn't even give us," she began. Our wedding gift had been a set of decorative pottery bowls. We had used a cardboard blender box to wrap our gift. Soon after the wedding, we had received a note from her based on the picture on the box instead of the actual gift inside.

When we received her first thank-you note, we smiled over her mistake because we know how easily something like this can happen. A few years ago, we bought several copies of a wonderful library book we had just read and gave these copies as Christmas gifts to several friends. A few days after Christmas, we decided to return our library book. That's when we discovered the only copy left was one of the new books. We presume one of our friends received an overdue library book as a Christmas gift. The library got the new copy. We were too embarrassed to ask around, so we hoped that the friend who wound up with the library copy kindly chalked this up as just a typical Cavera mistake.

Part of aging gracefully seems to be the ability to overlook much, to see with understanding, and to laugh at ourselves rather than to take life's small mistakes seriously. Eventually, even our faces seem to reflect whether we have chosen graciousness or judgment as a way of life. When we think of those older than ourselves, we know of faces that seem ready to smile and others that appear carved in stone hard misery. In *Tuesdays with Morrie*, author Mitch Albom's old professor urges him to "Forgive everybody everything." The act of forgiveness is a skill, like playing the piano or becoming a runner. The more we practice, the easier it becomes and the more we are able to accomplish increasingly difficult feats of forgiveness.

In these last days before a new year begins, one of the best places to begin our personal renewal might be to look through our past and make certain we hold no small grudges for trivial things. Then, we can move on to forgiving larger wrongs that truly matter. Ephesians 4:1–2 reminds us to "to lead a life worthy of the calling to which you have been called, with all humility and gentleness, with patience, bearing with one another in love…." Within our Christian community, this free-flowing, open forgiveness allows us to live in good-hearted gentleness and peace. The more we are willing to look past the faults of others, the better our outlook on life will be and the more at peace we will be within ourselves. The nature of this way of life has a name: grace.

Look Into the Future

One Saturday morning I (Jim) wheeled my ninety-year-old father down several long hallways to the chapel for Mass. We were newcomers to the St. Ann's Nursing Home Community. It had been less than a week since Dad's arrival from the hospital. Staff and residents greeted us warmly as we fell in line in an informal procession of wheelchairs and walkers. The gentle pace gave me an opportunity to admire the surroundings. Someone had taken time to wrap the pictures on the walls to resemble Christmas presents. We were told that they were to be opened after the holidays so that everyone could appreciate them all over again. I also noted small statues carefully placed in alcoves along the way. Most of them represented saints whose names had been familiar to me in my childhood. In some ways, I felt I was stepping back in time.

St. Ann's chapel was beautifully decorated for the Christmas season. We had arrived about ten minutes early, but already the side aisles were filling up with two rows of wheelchairs. Walkers could be found leaning against the ends of most of the pews. I manipulated Dad into an empty spot and found a place for myself in a nearby pew. We were a mixed group of staff, residents, and family members. Unlike my home parish, I was immediately aware that I was one of the youngest in the congregation. While coming into the chapel had felt like a step back in time, now I realized I was looking forward in time to my own future.

As the organ began to play, seven clergymen—one bishop and six priests, all residents—came forward to concelebrate the Mass. Three stood with some difficulty at the altar while the others were either in wheelchairs or used walkers. A casual observer might conclude that this was a very feeble group of Christians, an assumption far from the truth. The prayer, the music, and the whole atmosphere proclaimed the power of God. I was surrounded by a group of pilgrims whose faith was firmly grounded in God at the end of their journey. Though their voices may have sounded weak and their bodies appeared worn, their prayer remained strong and echoed confidence in a God close within their hearts. They prayed for the Church, for their families and for those in need. They voiced their unworthiness and asked for forgiveness. They came eagerly to the eucharistic banquet. At the conclusion of the Mass, we knelt in prayer as someone started those familiar words, "Saint Michael the Archangel, defend us in battle...." Though weak and worn, this community recognized that it still had work to do.

On that Saturday, I felt truly blessed to be part of the pilgrim church. I trust someday I will feel the closeness of God in my heart as I sit in the aisle in my own wheelchair praying for those in need.

Stargazers

Back in my (Jim) childhood years, the Christmas season started later and lasted longer. Our family decorated a fresh-cut pine tree around the Third Sunday of Advent. It remained in place until Epiphany. Today, decorated trees fill windows before Thanksgiving weekend. A few days after Christmas, the dried-out remains are tossed out by the curbs. No one seems to have time to wait around for the Magi to arrive with their gifts.

Often, when I see displays of the manger scene with shepherds and Wise Men crowded around the baby Jesus, I have a strong urge to announce to anyone within hearing that the arrangement is all wrong. I remember setting up our crib scene under the Christmas tree. Every piece had its proper place. We put the Wise Men and their colorful camels at the farthest point across the room. Each day my brothers and I moved the travelers a foot or so closer to the stable. Around the furniture and under the tables the figures gradually journeyed closer to the manger. On the twelfth day after Christmas, the travelers arrived and presented their precious gifts.

Scripture describes this group of foreigners as following a single star from a great distance. I always liked the Wise Men because their exotic clothes and large camels caught my imagination. As a child, I never really appreciated how difficult it must have been for them to follow a single star. Then, in the mid-1960s, when Ann and I lived as Peace Corp volunteers in a small village in West Africa, we had no electricity. At night we sat on our front porch and looked for constellations in the sky. Without the glare of electric lights, we discovered the wonder of the multitude of stars. We gained a new understanding of the wisdom it took for the Wise Men to find and focus on the one star that took them to Bethlehem.

We no longer seem to have time to stop and appreciate the sky at night. Even when we take the time to look up, few stars are visible to our eyes. Somehow, it seems appropriate that we can no longer see the stars because they have been dimmed by the light we have created. Yet, we are all still on a journey just as important as the one the Wise Men took, and we need a guiding star. Part of the wisdom of aging is a renewed effort to focus on the star, that light of Christ in our lives, that takes us in awe and wonder to the child in the manger.

Seeds of Faith

For Grandma Smith, the next big event after Christmas was the arrival of the seed catalogs. Even before we had the Christmas decorations packed away, a Gurney's seed catalog showed up in the mailbox. After Grandma left us for God's own garden, we have now become the "older folks" in our household. While we were thumbing through Gurney's, our younger daughter passed by and gave us her "Get a life" look. Here in bleak days of late December, we wistfully finger the pages with their promises of spring. On these pages, we are tempted by blackberries, day lilies, roses, asparagus, blueberries, grapes, and strawberries, all shown full-grown and ready to be enjoyed.

Buried deep in the middle of the catalog are a few other pages. These have small pictures of bug and rabbit repellants, weeding tools, sprayers, canning kits, apple parers, and grain grinders. Here we have hints of the hard labor actually involved if we are to bring the pictures on the covers to life. Blueberries and strawberries will not happen without a lot of digging, planting, and fertilizing.

The cold, dark days of winter are a good time to take a closer look at our spiritual growth. In Scripture, we find God's own seeds of faith, promises of new life, and pictures of glory. In fact, both the Old and New Testaments are filled with images of gardens, seeds, and sowers. We discover in Genesis that God intended for us to live our lives in a perfect garden. In Matthew 13:20–21, we are reminded that it is not enough to hear the word in passing. Rather, once the seed of the word is sown, we must allow roots to sink deep into the soil of our lives if our faith is to withstand hard times. A few verses later, we learn that the kingdom of heaven is like a mustard seed: small when it is first sown, but with enormous potential.

Within the pages of Scripture, we have the seeds of a faith-filled life. God, looking at this world, expects to find us sending down deep roots, blooming, and bearing fruit. Galatians 5:22–23 lists the fruits of the spirit as love, joy, peace, patience, kindness, generosity, faithfulness, gentleness, and self-control. Those of us who try to produce these fruits quickly understand that it takes a lot of spiritual digging, planting, and fertilizing to bring forth a good harvest in our souls. The days of Christmas are a time to remember that, if we expect to bring forth fruit in Christ, we must allow his word to sink its roots deep into our lives.

Unforgettable Christmas

Our Peace Corps duties in West Africa did not permit a trip after our wedding in 1966. Therefore, we decided to make our first Christmas together unforgettable. We booked passage on a luxury ship to the Canary Islands for the holidays. With great anticipation we often spoke of soft beds, hot showers, sunny beaches, and good food.

A few days before we were to leave, we invited some of our students over for an afternoon Christmas celebration. One of the boys came early and prepared traditional African foods: collard greens cooked in palm oil gravy with red peppers served over rice. For dessert, we had made several plates of Christmas ginger cookies. Among our students was a young man named Johnson. He stood tall and strong, even though he had lost one eye to infection. Because Johnson had often mentioned a younger brother, we asked him to bring his brother along to our dinner. At the appointed time, however, Johnson arrived without his brother. "Teacher, he will not come," Johnson explained. "He is ashamed because he does not know how to eat with a spoon." Knowing how much hunger our students suffered, we urged him to go back and get the younger boy. When he came back with his brother in tow, we gathered around our table. Johnson's brother shyly filled his plate and then found a place to himself where he ate in a fashion best suited to him. The boys ate all they could hold of their favorite foods and then quietly, hand-after-hand, reached for cookies until the plates were empty.

With appetites satisfied, the boys began to loosen up, alternating between English and their native Mano dialect. With much good-natured teasing and laughter, they shared things they found strange about us. One student told about the wonders he had seen in a German mining camp up the road. He claimed they had a pipe that made water come out inside the house! Who could believe such an outrageous thing? Now and then a large house spider scurried across the bare floor, causing a minor commotion. We had a deep sense of peace and joy among these children.

Anxious to begin our "real" Christmas celebration, the next morning we caught a ride to the capital city. Jim had not been feeling well, so we decided to make a quick stop by the Peace Corps medical office. His appetite had been poor, but I chalked it all up to my lack of cooking skills. It did not take long for the doctor to diagnose a major case of hepatitis and arrange for Jim to be placed in a bed at a clinic. For a brief moment, we thought that escaping on a cruise with sun and good food might be the healthiest alternative. Instead, Christmas for us became a room in a clinic with a small artificial tree on a table. Neither of us can recall much about the day at all. Later, we realized the unforgettable Christmas we wanted had been handed to us in the quiet afternoon we spent with our students. Peace, joy, love, laughter, feasting, and fellowship had fallen in our laps and we almost let it all pass without recognition.

In Bethlehem, hundreds of people passed by the real Christmas, hurrying on their way to something they imagined more important than a poor couple with a baby in a manger. Completely unaware, they missed the real Christmas that waited in their midst.

Living in the Word

Who doesn't like a good mystery on a cold winter night? Our older son rescued an abandoned family Bible from a dusty shelf in a store that sold used books. Printed in 1857, it is the few pages between the Old and New Testament that have captured my (Ann) attention. In a clear, bold script someone made a list of births, marriages, and deaths. As I study these dates, a story emerges. William Nagle was born on December 7, 1808. His wife, Elizabeth, first saw the light of day April 3, 1811. As children, William and Elizabeth might have heard firsthand tales of the American Revolution from their own grandparents. In due time, seventeen-year-old Elizabeth married William. By the time she turned forty-five, Elizabeth had given birth to six sons and six daughters, including a set of twins. Their second son, Charles, died just before his fifth birthday. Another son, John, died at the age of nineteen in May 1864. General Sherman began his march to Atlanta early that same year. Did young John lose his life marching south with Sherman? What more likely event might have caused the death of a nineteen-year-old son in the spring of 1864?

The final entries on the pages are the dates of death for William and Elizabeth. William died at the age of seventy-nine in 1888. Sturdy Elizabeth lived until 1897. The hand that wrote the dates signed his initials J.M.N. This youngest son, James M. Nagle, had enough faith to make certain his family would be remembered as long as this book existed.

Following this page of Nagle family history, the Gospel of Matthew begins with the words, "The book of the generation of Jesus Christ, the son of David, the son of Abraham." The next verses list the forefathers of the house of Joseph, husband of Mary. After Abraham came Jacob, who was himself the father of a large, imperfect family. Familiar names flow down through Obed, Jesse, and David. Next follows a line of others, many of whom I know little or nothing. Forty-two generations rose and fell before the birth of Christ. The Gospel of Matthew makes certain we remember. On a water-stained page at the back of this Bible someone has written a reference to Job 14. Out of curiosity I turned to the passage listed. The first verse is, "Man that is born of a woman is of a few days and full of trouble."

I think of all the struggling, imperfect families that have gone before us. Sometimes family members scratched small clues to whisper to generations beyond, "We were here." I wonder if these worn pages gave comfort to a mother or father late at night while a child fought in a trench in Germany, or on a ship in the South Pacific, or in Korea or Vietnam. Since time began, struggling families have written imperfect stories. Generation after generation, parents of faith kept vigil with an open Bible. Come war or famine, wealth or poverty, life or death, the word survives.

3
Lent

Create in me a clean heart, O God,
and put a new and right spirit within me.

PSALM 51:10

On the Road

For more years than we can remember, we have traveled to grandparents' homes with carloads of children. The northern route to my (Jim's) parents' home was one day each way while the southern route to Ann's parents' meant two days each way. Because of our busy work schedules, these two annual trips constituted our "vacations." To call them restful would be far from the truth. They provided us with a change of scenery, but the cost in mental and physical energy was so great that we literally had to have time to recover when we returned home. In spite of all the stress associated with these vacations, we found ways to make our travel time interesting.

We have always been a family of readers. We were regulars at the library and the staff was always friendly. They liked us so much that hardly a week went by when we did not get a letter from them! We had a longstanding family joke when the doorbell rang unexpectedly that it might be the "Library Police" coming to collect their overdue items.

Before every vacation, we headed over to our neighborhood library where each of us selected some personal books and Ann chose one for the family. At the start of each trip, in fact, as soon as we pulled out of the driveway, books and tapes emerged from each corner of the station wagon. Whenever the kids got restless or simply bored, Ann pulled out the family book and read to us while we sped through the countryside. We loved this part as our imaginations captured the words and phrases and painted glorious scenes, taking us far away from the drone of the engine and the bumps on the road.

On Ash Wednesday we began a journey with our Lord to Jerusalem. We know it will not be an easy journey, but we can be assured there will be some memorable moments. The scenery will include a barren desert where our deepest hungers will be confronted, a side trip up a mountain where we will be overwhelmed by a spectacular vision, and a long and winding road to the holy city, our destination. We will hear the word of God read to us and our imaginations will be filled with images of Abram looking up to the stars and Moses approaching a burning bush. We will come to understand the great compassion of God who gives us chance after chance to change our ways and follow his lead. And we will be in awe at the love of the father for the prodigal son and the mercy of our Lord with the woman caught in adultery.

Don't forget to take time along the way for some personal reading and prayerful reflection. And since our whole Church family is traveling together, feel free to share your thoughts and observations with one another. Lent is one of the most important stretches of the road on our journey together with God.

Fasting Together

With the start of Lent and the call to prayer, almsgiving, and fasting, I (Jim) was reminded of a family fast some years ago. Over thirty years ago my mother died. Prior to her death, she suffered the pain of cancer for a number of years, though she seldom talked about it. That was her way. Our family felt more and more helpless as we watched her suffer. Like many families, we were spread out over great distances, and most of us could not participate in her daily care.

One day I received a call from my brother Bob, who suggested that we have a family fast for Mother. His idea was that by all of us fasting for twenty-four hours on one particular day, we could, in a small way, share in the pain that Mother experienced every day. We all agreed to this plan, and a day was set. I remember it was a Tuesday.

Ann and I decided to feed the children as usual, but we would abstain from all solid food from after dinner on Monday until breakfast on Wednesday. On our fast day, we did all the things we usually did except eat. No one outside our family was aware of our project. Whenever I felt hungry, my thoughts turned to my mother. In midafternoon, Ann and I talked on the phone to check on our progress. We were both hungry, but that was OK. In the evening after we fed the kids and put them to bed, we talked about our day without food. We went to bed hungry that night, but more aware of our solidarity as a family.

Many of us seldom experience any physical hunger. We live comfortable lives and we take our comfort for granted. Even when we are spiritually hungry, there is much spiritual food available. Flyers for programs, retreats, and speakers arrive in our mail every week. We grab a spiritual snack or two at the first pang of emptiness. It is hard for us to comprehend the value of deep hunger in our search for God. We enjoy focusing on Scriptures that support our easy lives. Matthew 7:7 tells us, "Ask, and it will be given you...." We have gotten the asking and receiving part down to a fine art. The verse from Joel 2:12–13 is not used quite as often. Here God reminds us, "...[R]eturn to me with all your heart, / with fasting, with weeping, and with mourning; / rend your hearts and not your clothing."

We have no idea what it means to live in a Third World country where life is a constant fast. Even our understanding of the hidden poverty in our own cities is usually limited to occasional news coverage. True fasting creates a desert space in our comfortable lives. Especially in Lent we need to find a desert where we can be united with Christ who suffered and with all others who suffer and are truly hungry.

Time for Mending

Somewhere over the past decades we, as a nation, have lost the art of mending. There used to be whole professions dedicated to this task. Mending is a slow process and one that requires a lot of patience. It requires the mender to understand the brokenness and to see the loose fit, the empty spaces, and the missing piece. One must be willing to sacrifice precious time to study the problem and to envision possible solutions. Only then can the mending begin. In the end, wholeness is restored and something valuable is regained.

Today time has become too precious a commodity for the mending process. We simply dispose of broken objects and replace them with new ones. The "menders" have all but disappeared. Rarely do we find a craftsman who can repair a watch, mend a broken shoe, or fix a radio or small appliance. More and more often we are told that something is beyond repair.

The world says, "It will be cheaper to throw it away and get a new one."

In the second half of life, we have come to understand that many things are worth the time and effort required for mending. Friendships, family ties, marriages, and our relationship with God all take time and patience. We have to see the issues not only with our eyes but also with our hearts. In addition, we have to remember the past, revisit old wounds, forgive, and seek forgiveness. Mending is not easy. The world encourages us to let go of the old, move on, get over it, and find a new object of focus. Mending takes too long and, besides, there are no guarantees. Imagine what our world would look like if God went along with that line of thinking. Would any of us be here?

Lent is a season made for mending. The Scriptures call to mind God's faithfulness to his covenant with his people. The readings are full of images of suffering and betrayal alongside mercy and forgiveness. The question is, Will we "give up" some of our most precious time to mend fences? Can we distance ourselves from distractions long enough to understand our brokenness? Perhaps, like us, you will come up with a list of things left undone. Visits need to be made, letters need to be answered, and cards need to be sent. In short, a lot of relationship fences need mending. Making the list is too easy. The hard part is giving up the time for the mending. We can be assured that whatever time we give to mending will be worth it. During these forty days, God calls us, in the words of the prophet, to "Come back to me with all your heart." God waits for us to make our move. In the end, our wholeness can be restored if we take the time for mending.

Hearts on Straight

Our pastor describes Lent as "essential time," that is, a time to focus on what is essential in our lives. That term could also be applied to this stage of our lives. As Lent rolls around each year, we more often use it as a time for spiritual housecleaning in earnest—tossing out things we do not need in order to spiritually enrich who we are becoming. Our years of accumulated experiences have led to a realization that letting go is not an easy process, even when we are doing the choosing. Real change, the kind of change that this season calls for, is difficult. In the second half of life, we find ourselves wanting to cling to the things we have accumulated, to the lifestyle we have nurtured over time, and to our plans for the future—no matter how sketchy they might be. So we can understand the reluctance of Moses when God called him to lead the chosen people out of Egypt. Moses had reasons why God should find somebody else. Scripture reveals the mess that Moses had gotten into and how he was actually hiding out in the desert when God called to him from the burning bush. Leading a nation to freedom was not on his agenda. In the end, Moses let go and surrendered to God's plan.

Lent is about saying "yes" to God and being open to whatever he has in mind for us. It is about letting go of our focus so that we can be empty enough for God to fill our lives. In this spirit of "essential time" we have recently been trying to figure out the "nonnegotiables" in our own lives. What do we do that means so much to us we are willing to protect it at all costs?

The other day, Ann asked a friend about the nonnegotiables in her life. At first the friend named the big things: the generalities of faith and family that serve as the underpinnings in her life. Then Ann asked her to be more specific. What does she give away time for each week? What means so much she refuses to let anything else come between her and those moments? Our friend named two things: her work as a docent at the museum and her St. Vincent de Paul work on behalf of the poor. Her answer matched perfectly with who she is. The culture and ideas expressed in our museum are a match for a mind that treasures all that is good and beautiful in life. Her compassion for the poor is an expression of her good heart. "Why do you value these two things so much?" Ann asked. "Because they keep my heart on straight," she replied.

Fasting and praying in the essential time of Lent, each of us must discover what we need in life to "keep our hearts on straight."

Standing in the Stations

The Stations of the Cross have been a part of my (Jim) Lenten memories since childhood. As a child, I remember this devotion as being long and boring. It has only been in the second half of my life that I have come to appreciate the depth of the stations. The liturgy remains the same, but my perspective has changed. I rediscovered this devotion several years ago when I was preparing a talk on life journeys. I had been looking for resources when I came across a pamphlet for the Stations of the Cross for the sick. As I read this small pamphlet, it occurred to me that the stations are in many ways connected to my own life journey.

In the first station where Jesus is condemned to death, it is obvious that he was misunderstood and unfairly judged. I resent it when someone labels me and does not give me a chance. In spite of that, I know I have done the same thing to others.

I relate the carrying of the cross to my own personal burdens and responsibilities. Certainly mine cannot compare to our Lord's. Yet my burdens feel real and often overwhelming to me.

This insight helps me to appreciate even more the sacrifice of the cross.

Three of the stations are about falling down. Most of us have fallen and had to get up and face the consequences. The hardest part of falling down and getting up is that, in spite of our best efforts, it continues to happen. Just when we think we have it all together, a fall reminds us of our frail humanity. Jesus is with us in our falling down and our getting up.

The scene of Jesus meeting his mother speaks to me both as a parent and as a child. As I have grown older, I have become more aware of the fact that, like a child, I am quite dependent.

The stations where Simon helps Jesus carry the cross and Veronica wipes his face lead me to acknowledge that, after spending my life as a "giver," it is hard for me to receive help from others. If our Messiah could accept help and comfort from Simon and from Veronica, why can't I become a gracious receiver? These stations force me to look at why I have a need to be in control.

The scene of Jesus showing concern for the weeping women says to me that, even in the darkest of personal times, I must keep my sights on the needs of others rather than on my own misery.

The tenth station depicts Jesus being stripped of all that the world values: his good name, his dignity, even his only garment. What do material things mean when you get right down to it? Hospice patients can tell you that things accumulated in life mean little at the end. Often possessions blur our vision of truth and reality. Wisdom disguised as suffering can be a great teacher.

As with each of the other stations, I asked myself if I am part of the final ones depicting the crucifixion and death of our Lord and the laying of his body in the tomb. Accounts of a black man dragged to his death and a gay man brutally tortured and murdered remind us that crucifixion still happens. I do abhor the evil side of human nature, and I am disturbed by the realization that as a human I, too, am a part of this.

Looking carefully, I find my face in every station from the false accusations to the tomb.

Legacy

So, it all comes down to this. Last weekend Jim cleaned out "The Closet" under the basement stairs. This "bottomless pit" goes back under the stairs for about fifteen feet and then makes a sharp turn for additional forgotten storage. When my mother passed away, this closet became home for several boxes full of letters and cards she had saved from her friends.

Now, there are seven cardboard boxes next to my chair where they wait for what will be the final sorting of Mom's things: literally hundreds of letters, invitations, birthday cards, get well cards, and post cards from vacationing friends. Mom saved everything anybody ever wrote to her. When I occasionally suggested that we might be able to let go of some of the cards, she could not bear to think of it. After all, they were from her friends. "I might want to read what they wrote again," she said. Currently, I am making a separate pile to keep of all the letters I wrote to her, along with a few letters and pictures sent from our kids to Grandma and Grandpa. There is something about capturing a time and place on paper that creates a legacy from our hearts.

How is it that Mom's eighty-six years of life come down to these last seven boxes? The contents of these boxes are very much the contents of my mother's life. She was so focused on others that many of the letters begin with "Thank you so much for…." Whether the object of her thanks was a necklace, jars of home-made jam, a visit, or a wonderful letter, it is clear that Mom always found a way to give something to someone else.

Lent is about paring our lives down to the essentials. Eventually, after the clothes have been sent to St. Vincent de Paul and the furniture has been divided among the children, grandchildren, nieces, and nephews, life gets down to those last few boxes—the ones nobody wants to go through. How beautiful it will be if the contents of those boxes give testimony to how much we cared for other people. Sifting through my mother's letters makes me wonder. When my own children are faced with those last few cardboard boxes from my life, what will they find inside?

Hubcaps

Recently, I (Jim) discovered that my car is missing another hubcap. That makes two in the past six months. We do like to keep the pieces of this car together since it is our "good" one. With the first hubcap, I recalled running into a curb and retraced my route. No luck. A few weeks later, providence provided a hubcap near the church parking lot. No one claimed it. This hubcap didn't match my other three, but it fit perfectly and at least it covered the ugly wheel hub.

Then, a second hubcap turned up missing. Strangely, it was on the same side of the car, the passenger side, but this time it was the rear wheel. I tried to think where it might have popped off. On school days, I drive my daughter and her friend down a highway with lots of potholes. I made a note to myself to check out the roadside the next time I drove the kids to school.

One Sunday when we headed over to school for a music practice, I casually glanced out the passenger window and noticed a number of perfectly good hubcaps strewn along the side of the highway near those pesky potholes. I felt as though the hubcaps were calling my name. After dropping off my daughter, I went back to that stretch of road and pulled over. The first hubcap I picked up was badly dented and did not fit. A few hundred yards ahead, I found three more. These were very nice hubcaps from expensive cars and, sadly, all were too large for my little sedan. Suddenly, it dawned on me that people driving by were staring at me. There I stood on the side of the highway with a dejected look on my face, dressed in my Sunday best, as I clutched an armload of discarded hubcaps. I could not help but laugh at myself as I drove home.

How easy it is to get distracted and go off on a tangent. Jesus constantly reminded his followers to focus on the pillars of faith: love of God and love of neighbor. Even in Jesus' time, there were many distractions. The scribes and Pharisees focused on the rules. Jesus' closest disciples were caught up with their own egos, arguing about who would occupy places of honor in the kingdom. Many were convinced that the messiah would be a powerful king with strength to free the land from Roman occupation. Some had big ideas and some had small ideas, but they were all capable of being distracted from the way, the truth, and the light.

Human nature has a hard time staying focused. When I was a child, I got into staring contests with my brothers. The first one to blink, lost. Today, with the onslaught of information and instant communication, we do nothing but blink from one thing to another. As I write these words, I can almost imagine Jesus driving by and yelling at me, "Hey! What's my disciple doing over there picking up lost hubcaps? Get back on the road!"

Unexpected Gifts

From time to time, we like to think about, well...time. We do this even though it occurs to us that there is not a whole lot to be done about it. There is no way any one of us can change a single moment of the past or access a single moment of the future.

Forgiveness is the only tool we have for altering the past while the hope of unlimited possibility keeps us moving forward. Meanwhile, nothing really exists except whatever we create in the small bit of time currently sliding through our fingers.

Perhaps time is a concept we have created so that we can pretend we are in charge. We always think we can predict what the future holds. Yet God, who delights in surprises, keeps turning up in history at unexpected times and places. His creative wisdom and timing have worked some amazing wonders. For instance, the Scriptures often contain an element of surprise and unexpected timing. The Samaritan woman met Jesus at the well during the heat of the day. Most of the women drew water in the early morning or evening hours. As an outcast, this woman had probably been making her hot, lonely way to the well for years. She had little hope things in her life might change. Little did she know that at the most unexpected time and place she would encounter the One who would give her life meaning.

The man born blind spent his whole life sitting apart, listening as life passed him by. In spite of all those years of darkness, he waited with an expectant soul until he encountered the Christ who truly enabled him to see. When Lazarus fell ill, Mary and Martha confidently sent word for Jesus to come. They thought Jesus would hurry to them and heal Lazarus before he died. They waited. Jesus did not arrive as expected, and their brother died. Only then did God's timing bring about something far greater than either Mary or Martha or even poor Lazarus could have imagined. God always shows up, but seldom in the times or places we expect.

On Palm Sunday, Jesus made a triumphant entry into Jerusalem. Everybody rejoiced. The long-awaited Messiah had finally arrived, just as the prophets had predicted. Imagine the disappointment the crowd felt when they realized Jesus was not going to fulfill their image of a savior. God often sends us gifts, but seldom do those gifts fit our human expectations. God continues to work in our lives with a sense of surprise and timing that is far beyond human comprehension. It is the way of the world to quickly discard what cannot be understood. Our faith is centered on the gift the world discarded.

Christ still comes into our lives, wrapped in the bodies of the poor and sick. Often he appears disguised in crisis or illness, or the very people who cause us pain. How often we miss Christ when he shows up in a time and place we least expect to see him.

Ending the Drought

I (Ann) can still see my father in the final years of his life, standing with his hands clenched and his face dark with anger. He is telling us a story from his past that we have heard countless times. When the Great Depression hit in 1929, he and his older brother were thirteen and fifteen. As orphans, they had lived with a string of relatives, none of whom had made them feel loved or welcomed. One day, in a fit of rage, the boys packed their belongings and announced their departure. Their Aunt Minnie, with whom they lived at the time, never said a word to stop them. In stony silence, she watched them pack and let them go.

That story lurked just beneath my father's skin, waiting to erupt whenever one of life's many thorns pricked him. The climax of the story was always the same. "Well, I showed them! I got myself out of there. Nobody is ever going to treat me that way again."

As a child, his story frightened me. As a teenager, it made me angry. As a young mother, I felt bored and later embarrassed for him. Here in the second half of my own life, I feel only pity and sadness when I remember his story. You see, in all of those years,

I did not have the courage to tell him that he had never really left home at all. He had carried his relatives' indifference on his back for seventy years. To the end of his life, they still had enormous power over him, even though they had been dead and gone for decades. The hate he felt kept his soul parched for the love they could never give.

Here in Southern Indiana, we know what it is to go through a drought when farmers loose crops. Shrubs and small trees wither and die. The sound of wind whipping through the trees and the smell of rain in the air become vague memories. Even so, the drought in the land is nothing compared to the parched places we find in our human hearts. We cannot help but wonder what holds the floodgates of love closed.

It seems forgiveness is the key that opens those gates. In Luke 7, a woman saturated with love washed Jesus' feet with her tears and dried them with her hair. Jesus explained to the Pharisees that she poured out love because forgiveness had come into her life. As we have been forgiven, we are required to forgive others. Forgiveness received and passed on allows all of us to live freely in humble joy. It opens the gates so that love waters the parched places in our hearts. I wish I could have explained all of this to my father. Perhaps then, he would not have died a thirsty man.

Slice of Life

A few days ago, a friend offered us a reasonable explanation of why time seems to gain speed as we grow older. She said, "Think of it this way. Life is like a pie. When we are five years old, the whole pie can be divided into five big pieces. As the years go by, slices in the pie get smaller and smaller." By the time we are sixty-five, the same pie is being cut into sixty-five thin slices and the pieces get thinner every year. No wonder we ask where time went.

It is a struggle to get everything done when life slips through our fingers so quickly.

Recently we celebrated our twin granddaughters' first birthday. When they were born, we could hardly tell them apart. As far as time goes, their "pie" was still uncut. During the next few months, they became two very different girls. One is not shy at all and seems to thrive on excitement. The other, though friendly, is more introspective. Both are lovely and precious beyond words. While they have the whole pie of life before them, we keep trying to figure out how to stretch our little slices in order to spend more time in their company. Perhaps we cannot appreciate how precious a resource time is until it becomes scarce. Even our "long-range" plans now look ahead only five or ten years instead of the twenty or thirty years we counted forward in our youth.

Currently, we are trying to figure out how to use this little slice of time called Lent. Gone are the Lenten seasons where we promised to spend a large number of hours each week in spiritual disciplines, or to never slide into certain unhealthy patterns again. In fact, Lent comes around so swiftly that we just try to remember our unfinished business from last year and pick up where we left off. It is enough if we can make a little progress each year and manage to hold onto whatever gains we make.

In his book *Simplicity: The Freedom of Letting Go*, Richard Rohr states, "The small self must surrender to the great self. Otherwise, we get trapped inside of ourselves." Perhaps part of surrendering ourselves is about surrendering our time, too. As we surrender our ever decreasing slices of time to the great scheme of God's plan, we become connected within his larger picture. No matter how thin our slices get, when we keep the perspective of being part of infinity, the size of our slice matters less and less. How thin have the slices of your life become? Sometimes it seems as though ours are thin enough now that if we hold them up to the light, we can see eternity on the other side.

Shouting Hosannas

Grandma Smith lived alone in a house a block away from us after Grandpa's death a few summers ago. Through the first Christmas, she worked hard to write cards, keep up with family and friends, and take care of herself. After Christmas, we noticed it all became too much for her. We could almost see a cloud of depression descending over her shoulders.

A few weeks after Christmas, we had to face the question many in our generation will face: What are we to do when parents can no longer care for themselves? Grandma settled it all by telling us she either had to go to a nursing home or come live with us. We do have some fine nursing homes close by, and we knew she would be well-cared for in any one of them. Our final decision was based on the fact that my (Ann's) mother's mind had remained clear and she still had mobility. Her needs were simple and she enjoyed peace, quiet, and privacy, which was compatible with my desire to stay at home and write. Therefore, we decided to bring her into our house until we were no longer able to meet her needs.

Years ago, I dreaded the thought of that time. Like most of the things we dread, the product of our imagination is far worse than the reality when it arrives. Each day I matched my pace to her life. We made circular routes from her bed to the kitchen to her chair. When it came time to get ready for bed at night, she creamed her face and then held out her expensive jar of rose cream, a gift from a friend. "You take some, too," she insisted. We both creamed our hands, all the while taking whiffs of the rose scent. I straightened the covers around her, tucked her in, and kissed her forehead, just as she often did for me some fifty years ago.

On Palm Sunday, we celebrate our Lord's joyful entry into Jerusalem. I wonder if I would have been among the crowds shouting hosannas. Where were all those people when Jesus carried his cross to Calvary? Maybe it is still easier to welcome Christ from a distance than to hang around and get personally involved. When Christ rides into our lives with an aging parent, we want to welcome them with joyful hosannas, even though we know they are heading toward the valley of death. The summer we went through the last stages of cancer with Dad was not a pleasant trip. Even though Mom had lost some strength, when she came to live with us she still had a grace and dignity I envied. She spent much of her time in prayer. She gently, almost eagerly, made her way through the valley where she knew Christ and Dad would meet her at the end. While she lived with us, we sang hosannas and our home was filled with peace and joy. During the difficult, dark days as she neared her death, we prayed for courage not to flee and for the strength to continue to walk with love and devotion by her side.

4

Holy Week/Triduum

"Remain here, and stay awake with me."
MATTHEW 26:38

Take This Cup

A friend of ours recently became a eucharistic minister. She told us how deeply moved she was the first time she served as minister of the Blood of Christ. We replied that even as eucharistic ministers for many years, the power of this moment still has a profound effect on us. The understanding of this ministry as God's holy work never fades.

Recently, as a minister of the cup, I (Ann) noticed something. The cup was lifted and there was a brief moment of recognition as the words "The blood of Christ" were spoken. As the cup passed to the hands of the receiver, I remembered the hands of Christ. With his hands, Christ touched the leper and cured him. Through the hands of Christ, the blind received sight. When Peter lost faith and began to sink beneath the waves, Christ stretched out his hand to restore him. At the Transfiguration, the hand of Christ touched the shoulders of Peter, James, and John and called them back to the reality of their work. Parents brought children to Jesus for his touch, his blessing, and his prayer. With his hands, Christ broke the bread and lifted the cup. Finally, the same hands

that served, saved, and healed were nailed to the cross in crucifixion.

This Holy Week, I am struck by how much the hands reaching for the cup have become the hands of Christ. A recently en-
gaged young woman comes with a new diamond sparkling on
her hand. As she takes the Blood of Christ, I pray that her love
and marriage will shine with strength and beauty fifty years from
this moment. Some of the hands that reach for the cup are gnarled
and tremble with age. For those with Parkinson's disease or ar-
thritis, I pray for health and strength. Here is the physician who
cared so well for my father when he had cancer. God, bless his
gift of caring and healing. Beautifully manicured nails and a finger with a large emerald ring grasp the stem of the cup. I know
this woman. She has been blessed with abundance, yet her heart
is one of service to the poor. I know she gives away much of what
she has. God, bless her kindness. Children come in the arms of
parents. With a brief touch they are given a prayer for Christ's
peace and joy in their lives. The workman comes, hands calloused,
nails broken. In line are the chef, the teacher, the beautician, and
the accountant. By their hands, they live their faith.

This day, millions of faithful hands reach for the cup. The
same hands receiving the Body and Blood have become the hands
of Christ. Do we really comprehend the power in the phrase
"handing on the faith"? It is through our hands that the presence
of Christ becomes a reality in the lives of others.

Images of Christ

In a dark hallway at a local nursing home, I (Ann) walked past
an elderly woman in a wheelchair. She noticed my camera and
asked me to take her picture. As I lifted my camera, she held up

a large birthday card and explained that the card was from her son and that she wanted to send him a picture of herself. I had been taking pictures outdoors and did not have a flash attachment with me. There was not enough light in the hallway to take any kind of picture. She looked so hopeful, so glad to seize this moment, that I opened the lens and shot without explaining the picture had no possibility of turning out well. Yet when the pictures were developed, hers was there. Every wrinkle, freckle, and mole stood out crisp and clear on the face of a mother smiling for her son.

A few days later I returned to the nursing home with my pictures. The administrator looked them over and paused when she came to the woman holding the card. Quietly the administrator said, "She passed." Her comment caught me off guard. "Died a couple of days ago," she continued. When I explained that the woman had wanted the picture for her son, the administrator promised to send it to him. All I ever knew of the woman in the wheelchair came from a brief encounter and a fortunate shot with the camera. Most of what we know about one another comes from images caught in brief encounters.

The painted images of Christ on the cross are among the most familiar in the world. We see the horror of those hours and know that the reality of crucifixion is beyond our comprehension. We forget that, along with physical crucifixion, Christ also endured the crucifixion of being abandoned by most of those whom he loved. Although on Palm Sunday, Jesus triumphantly entered Jerusalem to shouts of "Hosanna!" and waving palm branches, within a few days, the cheering crowd was replaced by an angry mob. He was betrayed by one of his closest companions and deserted by the rest. No image exists of this inner crucifixion of Christ by those who knew him best.

We become one with Christ when we experience betrayal,

disloyalty, and desertion. When we must watch helplessly while someone we love suffers, we stand at the foot of the cross with Mary. Even as we write this article, the phone rings. A friend tells me that her father has fallen...again. She has just spent hours with him in the emergency room...again. I listen while she shares how painful it is to walk this dark path with her beloved parent. I tell her that those who are willing to say "yes" to crosses such as these are experiencing the invisible crucifixion of Christ. It is Holy Week, and I remind her that she is sharing in Christ's crucifixion.

I believe only those who are willing to take up such crosses also emerge in a resurrection of peace and joy that others cannot comprehend. Does my friend see the experiences of sharing in Christ's crucifixion as the grace-filled moments that they are? Perhaps not now. The images being imprinted on her heart have not had time to develop. Even though for the present time the images remain obscure, I pray that they will become clear as they are brought into the light of the Risen Christ, a light beyond our comprehension, a light that can create a clear image even in the darkest hallway.

Holding a Foot

In the mid-1960s, we set off to West Africa where we taught school as Peace Corps volunteers. Over the years, we continue to have fond memories of that adventure in our lives. Recently, while discussing different types of prayer, a phrase our African students often used came back to us. When they needed something, they often wrote a short letter to us. Then, either the student or a friend quietly slipped us the carefully folded note. We learned not to immediately acknowledge receiving the note but to wait and read it in private. These requests for assistance had a definite pattern to them. They began with an apology for having to bother us. That was followed by the story of their particular need. They always concluded with the phrase "Teacher, I hold your foot"—a phrase indicating a posture of profound humility and deep entreaty. Common at the time, this phrase would be repeated with expressions of gratitude.

The simplicity and honesty of these notes deeply touched us. For years one of us carried one of these notes to remind us of how little we know of hardship. This note said simply, "Teacher, I have not eaten in two days. Do you have work I can do to earn money for food?" Who could not be moved by a young man "holding our feet" in this way?

The image of a person bent low to the ground, pleading while holding onto someone's feet, is a powerful image of humility and prayer in a time of deep need. Matthew, Mark, and Luke each record our Lord's agony in the Garden of Gethsemane. Christ prayed that the cup before him might pass him by if possible. He prayed in such agony that it was as if he bent low and held his Father's feet. Yet within this prayer was a deeper desire. Above all else, Jesus asked that his Father's will and not his own be done. Jesus' deepest desire was for his Father's plan to be fulfilled, regardless of the cost to him.

Fortunately, most of us have to "hold our Father's feet" only a few times in life. If a child runs away, or a husband or wife has cancer, or a parent has Alzheimer's, our hearts break and we bend so low to the ground that we hold God's feet in prayer. Around us is a dark garden between our prayer of desperation and the light of God's will. Christ's unshakable commitment took him out of the Garden of Gethsemane to continue on God's path for his life. Only by faith can we let go of our Lord's feet and leave our own dark gardens with a sense of peace in his will.

"Jerusalem, My Destiny"

On Ash Wednesday, we received a reminder of the true nature of our humanity. With a smudgy splotch on the forehead, we declared our faith and entered into the journey to Jerusalem. Did we really choose to join in or was it thrust upon us because, as the song says, this journey is our destiny? That is a question worth pondering. What we do know is that over these past weeks, we have been to a desert of temptation, to the mountain with a vision, and we have spoken to a Samaritan woman beside an ancient well. We have crossed the healing path of a man born blind and stood in awe as a dead man was called out of this tomb. We have been a witness to power and simplicity, to honesty and disbelief, to wonder and fear, to gratitude and tears.

These encounters have filled our minds with questions. Where do we stand in the crowd waiting at the gates of Jerusalem? Did we leave some time ago with the rich young man? Are we in a back room somewhere with a group of Pharisees trying to decide how to get rid of this man who has so little regard for the law? Or, have we come far enough on our journey to receive the new sight of faith? Are we walking with the Samaritan woman after she left her water jug and her unclean life at the well? Like the tax collectors, do we finally see that it is not about money after all? Or, with the thief on the cross, are we just humbly begging for mercy to enter the gates covered only with the grace of Christ?

Today we find ourselves at the gates of the great city where the faith we developed on our journey will be put to the test. Soon our ears will be filled with hosannas as the crowds open their arms in welcome: "Blessed is he who comes in the name of the Lord." What a glorious and triumphal beginning for our Master and for all of us on the journey! Yet in a short time, the joy-filled singing will turn into angry cries of death and crucifixion.

The hands that waved palms will soon be tightly clasped around swords and spears and whips. We ask how this could happen. Yet, through it all, Jesus holds steady, teaching us how to live, how to remember, and how to die.

It is Holy Week. There is no greater week throughout the year. It is a time for reflection on the word in the gospels. It is a time for coming together as a worship community to witness and participate in the moments that have affected our lives as followers of Christ. It is a time to share the stories of these sacred days in the holy city with those young and old gathered around our tables. It is a time to stop and focus on the truth of Jesus Christ in our lives. It is a time to forgive, to ask for forgiveness, to pray "Jesus, remember me when you come into your kingdom." Jerusalem is our destiny.

Riddle of the Cross

Mom Cavera started a family tradition as a way of putting some extra fun into Easter morning. My brothers and I (Jim) had become bored with hunting for colored hard-boiled eggs, so Mom created a series of notes. Each one contained a set of directions eventually leading us to our hidden baskets of goodies. We had great fun carefully studying her notes and running through the house. If we did not know right from left or had no sense of direction, we were in trouble. Mom and Dad laughed when we crashed into each other or headed off in the wrong direction. Fortunately, we knew we could always count on them for help getting back on track.

Years later, I carried on the same tradition with our four children. Instead of directions, I wrote a series of clues in riddle form to be solved. Our kids loved the challenge as much as I did when I was their age. The clue "Hidden under the chair where you sit three times a day" meant they would find a clue taped beneath their chairs at the kitchen table. While Ann and I pulled the covers a little tighter under our chins, we hoped the clues were easy enough for them to figure out by themselves but hard enough to keep them busy for a while. The older they got, the more difficult it became to keep the game going. By the time they were nine or ten, I often did not get to bed until midnight or later trying to keep the clues interesting. Still, for many years these hunts ended with a loaded Easter basket discovered in the clothes dryer or deep in a closet or behind a sofa. For the children, the journey was as much fun as reaching their goal.

Though Easter baskets are not central to our Easter celebration, the joy of discovery is. Certainly the disciples had clues to Jesus' death, but it took the joy of discovery on Easter morning to open their hearts to the resurrection. On Monday morning of Holy Week, we walked with a small group of people carrying a large wooden cross through the downtown business district. We walked slowly, singing hymns. Stopping at several places along the way including the Rescue Mission and the jail, we prayed for those who were brokenhearted, lonely, or in need. For many of those along the street as we passed, the cross is still a riddle. Some people reacted with puzzled expressions. Others looked away. Others smiled and nodded. People react differently to the cross. Those of us walking together wanted only a quiet opportunity to share the central mystery of our lives.

The path through Holy Week is familiar to us as we anticipate the joy of Easter morning. Too often the world rushes past. Everyone is looking for a personal basket of goodies. Compelling us to slow down and reflect, the riddle of the cross asks us a number of questions. What does it mean that Jesus suffered and died for you? What is it that you seek in Jerusalem? Will you find what you are looking for at the end of your journey?

5

Easter

*"And remember, I am with you always,
to the end of the age."*

MATTHEW 28:20

An Entry From a Deacon's Diary

It is Easter Sunday night, and I (Jim) find myself utterly exhausted as I sit in my recliner with a magazine and notepad on my lap. Our younger daughter left to return to college several hours ago. The house is quiet. Ann is downstairs on the computer completing an assignment she has due tomorrow. In spite of my weariness, I feel spiritually energized from the many beautiful, prayerful experiences of Holy Week. My mind lingers over the haunting words of the good thief that we sang on Good Friday: "Jesus remember me when you come into your kingdom." I recall the light, hope, and joy in the faces of the newly baptized at the Easter Vigil. My favorite image is of a group of children gathered on Easter morning in a large room in our ministry center. Dressed in their best clothes, several clutched small empty baskets while they waited to begin the Easter egg hunt out in the yard. While the parents exchanged pleasantries, the children moved toward boxes of toys in the corner of the room. Within a

few minutes their imaginations stirred and they began to build a
wall from cardboard bricks. Our almost-grown daughter moved
in and around the groups of children to capture Easter images
with our camera. I kept thinking how blessed we have been on
this Easter day.

I sink deeper in my recliner and pick up some mail I had set
aside for a time such as this. Among the periodicals is the spring
issue of *Lifelines*, a publication from the international adoption
agency through which we were blessed with our youngest child.
Each issue of *Lifelines* has a section devoted to photographs of
happy-faced children from around the world who have found
new homes in towns and cities throughout the Midwest. Each
issue also has a section called "Children of Promise," which fea-
tures photographs and descriptions of children from Eastern Eu-
rope, Asia, and Latin America who are waiting to be adopted.
Many have handicaps, and a number are siblings. Some are simply labeled "older and healthy." My eyes move slowly across the
page, taking in each facial expression, date of birth, and brief
description. I try to imagine what each child might be thinking
and what it would mean to have one of these children come into
my life. Would he or she love me?

I cannot help but wonder if God does this with us, his adopted
children. Does he imagine our potential and wonder if we will
love him after he has blessed us with unconditional love? After
God's gift of Easter, how could we not love him?

Beyond Doubt

Thomas was not the first to doubt. Sarah, old enough to know
better than to doubt the Lord, listened from behind the tent flap
and laughed at the news of God's plan for her. Age had taught
her the facts of life and to be practical. Obviously, she was too

old to bear a child. Age had also closed her mind to the unlimited possibilities of life in the company of the Lord. In the beginning, Moses did nothing but question the Lord of the universe. What would he say when Pharaoh asked who sent him? Perhaps God had forgotten that he could not speak very well. Couldn't God send someone else? Moses felt he was the mistake in God's plan.

The angel of the Lord found poor, timid Gideon cowering inside his winepress trying to thresh his wheat. Gideon reminded the angel that he was the least powerful person in a weak family. Surely, God had no use for him. Every year we have the story of doubting Thomas on the Sunday after Easter. As we age in faith, many of us also still have our doubts. This story of Thomas is for all of us who struggle to overcome doubts as we continue to try to grow in faith. The commentators often describe Thomas as struggling to believe, and who could blame him? Jesus coming back from death—by crucifixion, no less—well, this was too much for poor Thomas to swallow. When we read this in the gospel, we are convinced that not only was it written for us, it also describes us. As people of the most technologically advanced nation on earth, we demand proof. We love our sciences and we have grown to depend on them to provide answers to all of life's problems. Science tells us that when we are dead, we are dead. At heart, Thomas was like a modern American. He wanted real facts he could touch and see. He needed to experience the risen Christ for himself. Jesus obliged him with a direct encounter. It took the experience of Jesus alive and present to confirm Thomas' faith.

Doubts often come with physical decline. Will we have enough in the way of resources to buy medicine and food? Will we die of illness or alone? And what about our children? Do they care about what is happening to us? Are the best years in life over? Does God still have use for us, or is it downhill all the way?

Most of us don't have the courage of David. It is difficult to try to slay the giants waiting at this point in our lives. We don't have the faith of Joshua, the loyalty of Ruth, or the humility of Mary, who asked only that the Lord's will be done in her life. We are painfully aware that our faith is sometimes less than what we had hoped it might have become by now. Sometimes the best we can do is stand in the company of our doubts and wait for the Lord to appear in whatever room we have locked ourselves into. Christ invites us to put our fingers into the nail prints in his hands. We join our experience to his. His courage and humility become ours, and we discover, as did Sarah in old age, that nothing is impossible with the Lord.

Redemption

A cousin of ours lives in Lexington, Kentucky. Danny is a man with a heart of gold who lives a rough-and-tumble life on his own terms. He is also an excellent artisan who makes his living etching glass for partitions in fancy restaurants and banks. He runs his business from a house near the inner city of Lexington. He never bothers to take the keys out of the ignition of the large, old truck that he parks outside his house.

Late one night, Danny heard somebody drive away with his truck. He ran into the dark too late to catch the thief, and so he filed a police report. Thinking the thief might not have gone too far, Danny spent the next couple of days driving around the inner city. Sure enough, he spotted his truck parked beside the curb down a dead-end street. He quickly summoned a police officer to verify his stolen property. Inside the cab of the truck he found two things: a man's size 4X jacket and a humongous pair of almost-new, hardly worn work boots. He made two decisions on the spot. First, Danny decided not to prosecute the thief—after all, he had left the keys in the ignition. Second, since he was not going to prosecute, the officer would not even have to go to the trouble of knocking on doors trying to locate the perpetrator.

Danny had his truck back, but what was to be done with the jacket and boots? Giving them to a large-size friend to wear around the streets of Lexington would not be a favor to anyone. The jacket went to Goodwill. We happened to be visiting in Lexington and mentioned our parish project to supply good, used shoes for the homeless. The large, almost-new work boots came home with us and joined the growing pile to be donated to a shelter after Easter.

Those boots are a "perfect fit" with Easter, which is about trading old lives for new. Our hope is not in what we do, or who we are, but in the resurrection. Because of Easter, we are able to trade our old lives for new life in Christ. We walk away from the empty tomb knowing that Christ, freed from death, has freed us from death, too. It seems fitting that boots belonging to the thief will find their way onto the feet of the homeless. From the negative experience of a robbery, good—and new life—will come. Furthermore, when it comes to salvation, aren't we all thieves and homeless? Aren't all of us trying to steal into heaven by walking in the shoes of Christ?

Resurrection: Pass It On

We have come through Lent and gone past Easter morning. Here on the "other side" of Easter, there is plenty of encouragement to live a resurrection life. We have thrown open windows to take full advantage of bird songs and fresh air. Cans of fresh paint are waiting in the basement, and flats of flowers by the front door are ready to be planted.

Yet in the middle of new life represented by flowers and birds, many of us still have patches of winter in our hearts. Grief over a son or daughter who continues destructive behavior or the perpetual unkindness of a brother or sister can leave cold crevices in our souls where spring never comes.

Grandma Smith had a special gift with plants and flowers. She loved them, and it showed in the way she cared for them. In her younger years, she had a yard filled with beautiful blooms. In her last years, small pots crowded the windowsill in her room. We often brought our own sickly, failing potted plants to her. She carefully looked them over and told us to leave them with her for a while. Weeks later she delighted in showing us how they had been rejuvenated. In fact, she often stopped us from throwing out a plant we judged to be compost material. She always wanted to try a few things that might bring them back. And bring them back she did. In her hands, they revived and grew stronger and more beautiful than ever.

Grandma was a plant rehabilitation specialist. In addition to the resurrection, Easter was a special season for Grandma because of the joy she found in the bursting forth of trees and flowers. In the same way Grandma brought forth new life in plants, Jesus called forth new life in people. You might say he was a people rehabilitation specialist. This was true not only for those he encountered once but also for those with whom he spent a lot of time. In spite of their many failings, Jesus did not abandon his apostles and bring on a new crew.

A notable example of this was Jesus' treatment of Peter. After the resurrection, Peter went running to the empty tomb. On Lake Tiberias, Peter jumped from the boat and swam to meet Jesus on the shore. He appeared anxious to have his relationship with Christ restored, yet he seemed so ashamed of himself he could hardly look Jesus in the eye. John's Gospel tells us that, after the resurrection, Jesus asked Peter three times if he loved him (21:15–17). Many commentaries speak about this passage as being the gospel writer's way of saying that, in spite of Peter's denials, Jesus did not write him off. Instead of making Peter grovel, Jesus took the first step to restore the relationship. As a people rehabilitation specialist, the resurrected Christ sought to give Peter new life and to restore his dignity.

When people need our love and forgiveness, who are we to withhold the resurrection?

Not Looking Back

In the days following Easter, it often feels as though we have gone backward in time. Trees are in full bloom along with tulips. Azaleas are almost open. However, the weather seems to be mixed up. We had to dig out coats and hats for our walk this morning. A cold wind blew from the north while clouds overhead spit snow-flakes. Both of us have been looking forward to the days after Easter. Instead we seem stuck back in the days of Lent.

As Christians, we often behave much like the weather. During Lent, we bloom a little, make steps toward a new season, and appear to be changing and making progress. Finally, we lose a few pounds, exercise a little more frequently, spend more time in prayer, and work a little harder at spreading kindness and peace. After Easter, instead of continuing to live a resurrected life, we drift back to where we were before Lent began. A friend of ours put things in perspective when she said, "What good is Lent if we just look forward to getting back to where we were?"

Have we really allowed the days of Lent and the joy of Easter to transform our lives? Recently, we saw an example of a life-changing transformation in our son Chris' life. When our grand-daughters came into this world, our son and his wife entered the new kingdom of parenthood. When their twin daughters were born, he called us from the delivery room. Like Peter at the empty tomb, he was amazed and overwhelmed. His comment to us was that he was certain there are no atheists in foxholes or delivery rooms.

In much the same way, the empty tomb is our delivery room, calling us to life in God's new kingdom. Just as everyone who encountered the risen Christ was transformed, when we encounter the risen Christ of Easter, we are faced with an opportunity to allow transformation to take place in our own lives. This means letting the journey we made during Lent become a well-worn path we continue to follow. To go forward in the spirit of Easter, we need to ask ourselves if there is anything still keeping us in the tomb. Is there someone we have not forgiven or someone in our lives we are refusing to love? Are we still buried in some guilt and shame that keeps the dawn from breaking in our own lives?

Looking forward to getting back to where we were robs us of the joy of Easter. Letting go and making room for the resurrection in our lives allows Easter to continue to bloom in our hearts. Choosing to live a life resurrected by love makes Christ visible in a world that desperately needs to experience new life.

Joy of Communion

Last Sunday after Mass, I (Jim) sat down beside a friend and her eighteen-year-old niece Andrea at a table in our fellowship hall. As we talked, my friend mentioned that today would be Andrea's last day in town. I knew her niece had enlisted in the Navy and was scheduled to report in early fall. Meanwhile, Andrea had recently rejoined our community, renewing her faith in preparation for this next step in her life. However, in these days of conflict and bloodshed in far-off lands, Andrea had just been "called up" early and was to leave for training the next day.

This past Sunday was also first Communion day for seven

children in our parish. After Mass, they stood before the congregation and sang, "Like a shepherd he leads his flock...," and their soft, clear voices spread over all of us. Now, at a nearby table, these same children were eating cake and opening small gifts. As the girls in their white dresses laughed with the joy of their celebration, their small hands peeled open boxes containing new rosaries and small crosses.

Sitting on my left, Andrea caught me off-guard when she began recalling her own first Communion Sunday in our church some ten years earlier. I guess I had forgotten that reminiscing is not the exclusive prerogative of us "older folks." I wondered if, in a way, she was saying goodbye to a time when she experienced the initial joy of God's love and the love of her parents at her own first Communion celebration.

The space between first Communion and a young adult's first step into the larger world is so brief: normally ten short years. Within the next ten years, these children just now receiving first Communion must begin to know and appreciate their gifts. They must understand both the dangers and opportunities in the world, learn to temper love with wisdom, rise above the pain that comes from living with an open heart, and know the power of forgiveness and the joy of being forgiven. Even a lifetime is not enough to accomplish so much. In ten short years, the best parents and a faith community can hope to do together is lay a strong foundation.

Meanwhile, we are bound together regardless of time and space by the power of the Eucharist. Whether our children leave us for college campuses or unknown assignments in distant countries, faith provides a way to unite us in love. Through the Eucharist, we remain one in Christ and are strengthened for whatever life brings us. No matter where our lives take us, we are always safely at home in the Eucharist.

It is not an easy world that awaits our children. We pray that the children at the table next to us will continue to grow in grace and love. As older parents of grown children, we also pray that Andrea will carry the joy of Communion with her, that she will be united with us and strengthened every time she extends her hands to receive our Lord in the Eucharist.

Thanks, Mom!

In the middle of spring weather, the beautiful blossoms, the end of another school year, first Communions, and the promise of long summer days, we stop to celebrate our mothers. For many of us in the second half of life, we take this time to recall our growing-up years when our mothers were so much a part of our lives.

Recently, we asked several people to share any special memories they had of their mothers. One ninety-one-year-old woman's favorite memory was of seeing her mother stand up in church and sing a duet with another woman. Another friend of ours recalled staying out long past curfew one night during her teenage years. When she finally came home in the wee hours of the morning, the girl had to sneak past her mother's bed to get to her own. The mother had been waiting up, snacking on a banana while watching for her daughter. When she saw her daughter coming up the walk, the mother quickly jumped into her own bed and pretended to be asleep. The daughter thought she had made it when the mother, fully clothed—even wearing shoes and a coat—sprang from the bed, grabbed her daughter, and began beating her...with a banana peel. What might have been a moment of fury and anger turned into laughter.

When Ann reflects on her own gentle mother, she remembers her wearing a sunbonnet, standing in the garden, and vigorously wielding a hoe to dispatch an unfortunate snake. Jim's mother had a unique way of waking him and his brothers for school. She often took the broom handle and banged it on the ceiling directly under their beds. She did not stop until she heard the sound of their feet hitting the floor. Saturday mornings were different. She let them sleep until ten o'clock and then came into their bedrooms and ran the vacuum cleaner until they got up.

Moms live heroic lives. They often work both inside and outside the home as they struggle to stay afloat in both places. While dreaming of wonderful futures for their children, moms do what is necessary when it comes to getting children out of bed, putting food on the table, and working beyond the meaning of "tired." More than any other calling, motherhood is a direct connection with the heart of God.

Many of us are fortunate enough to remember our mothers as women of prayer. Those prayers were the insurance policies that covered us when we put ourselves in harm's way. Prayer opened doors for us and accompanied us into places we could not have walked alone. Our mothers' prayers kept us safe in God's hands when we were out of hers and brought us home like a lifeline in the night. What mother of teens has not kept vigil past curfew and prayed until the child came home, at which point she "pretended" to be asleep? What mother hasn't been ready to go out into the dark to find an out-past-curfew teen and, if necessary, beat him or her up with a banana peel?

Something for Nothing

In our later years, little memories often bubble up like small underground springs. Events that seemed insignificant when they occurred sometimes mean a great deal later in life.

Our backyard cherry tree is one such memory. At age seven,

our older daughter Katie became enchanted with plants. Seed catalogs bearing her name began arriving early in March. She sent away for whatever pictures looked the prettiest. Every summer she grew something different...until she discovered herbs. Before long, various mints in ragged clumps consumed a sizable portion of the backyard. For years, the smell of mint hung heavy every time we mowed. One spring, a two-foot tall cherry tree came as a free gift with her catalog order. She busied herself outside and soon called us to see where she had planted her tree. We couldn't bring ourselves to tell her that she had made a mistake planting a cherry tree in the tight corner formed by the back wall of the house and the outside basement stairwell. We figured the free, spindly tree probably would not last the summer, and so for the joy of the moment, we held our tongues. The memory of Katie at age nine—sweaty, hands grubby, blond hair sticking to her neck, and a proud smile on her face—remains with us.

Katie grew and so did the tree. When she entered high school, the branches reached just below our second story bedroom window. By the time she graduated and left for college, her tree stretched above our bedroom window and made a canopy over the stairwell. Its branches announced the arrival of spring with thousands of dainty white blossoms. When Katie graced us with her happy presence in the summers, we picked cherries together and made her favorite pie.

Now, years later, Katie has married and moved far away. Her tree has completely taken over the corner between our back wall and the outside stairwell. When winter winds blow, small, ice-covered twigs scrape against our house at night. From our window, we watch bees collect nectar in the spring. As we write this, hundreds of full, ripe cherries shine among the leaves. Yesterday, we picked and froze enough to make a couple of pies whenever Katie makes it home. We peer from our window, eye-to-eye with birds making a feast of the rest of the fruit. The tree that came without price has become priceless. It has never been sprayed or fertilized, yet it has returned a thousand-fold of joy for all of the "nothing" we have provided.

It is a rare thing to be able to continue to give abundantly for little or nothing in return. The cherry tree is like many of our fathers who, year after year, pour out their love and devotion by quietly working to provide for their families. Happy Father's Day to all of our dads who give so much and expect little or nothing in return.

Breaking Free

By the time we are more than halfway down the road of life, time becomes a precious commodity. We hoard the years we think we have left as though time has become water in a canteen for a trip across the desert. Do we have enough to make it from one oasis to the next? Is there enough time left to make it to a grandchild's graduation or wedding? What about our golden wedding anniversary? Will we have time enough down the road to see the birth of a great-grandchild? All the while we hope not to drink from any wells that have been poisoned by disease.

This thing we call time is a curious commodity. Thankfully, we know that it will not bind us in heaven. For that matter, sometimes it does not bind us on earth, either. Not long ago, our daughter and son-in-law came from California and spent a precious six hours with us. Never mind the circumstances. A six-hour window of opportunity opened for them and they took it. We crammed six weeks of hugs, laughter, and conversation into those six hours. The time passed so quickly that it seemed no more than six minutes. We lived each minute in those six hours so fully that time beyond the moment ceased to exist.

Our Lord's death and resurrection broke through human history in a way that makes time no longer relevant. Easter is the reality of salvation breaking through time the same way that seeds break through earth's crust into the light. The roots of some plants—like carrots, onions, sweet potatoes, and even peanuts—bear fruit underground. Whether we think of ourselves as a sweet potato, onion, or even a lowly peanut, we, too, must still bear fruit within this soil we call time. All the while, the green, growing, thriving part of the plant (that is, our spiritual life) flourishes in the light above without being trapped by the earth (that is, time) at all.

Now and for all eternity, Christ's death and resurrection have freed us from time. When our troubled souls grasp the meaning of the resurrection, we are standing with the women beside the open tomb. Our hearts feel the same love, wonder, and gratitude that overwhelmed their hearts, and we run with them eager to spread the news. Time ceases to exist. The only time that matters now is God's time. Alleluia!

6

The Road to Emmaus

And he said to them, "What are you discussing with each other while you walk along?"

What Are We Doing Here?

On September 6, 2001, we flew to Los Angeles to visit our daughter and son-in-law. Of course, we had no idea then of the national tragedy that would strike on the day we were due to fly home. Since September 11, 2001, we have been reviewing our own lives in an effort to renew our commitment to Christ. Many other people have told us they are in the same position. As it turned out, the young man who sat down beside Ann on our flight to California turned out to be "John the Baptist" for her. He made her reflect upon how she could be a more powerful witness to the saving presence of Christ in her life. She began writing the following essay the day after we landed in Los Angeles.

Early yesterday morning a small propeller plane allowed us to hop over the Appalachian Mountains and walk into the Atlanta airport. Soon we boarded a huge, crowded jet bound for Los Angeles. The passenger sitting next to me turned out to be a tanned young man who obviously spent a lot of time in a gym. The five diamond-studded earrings in one ear and the barbed wire tattoo around his biceps were signals that, if he wanted to talk, it could be an interesting flight. "John" turned out to be a carpet-layer and a personal trainer from West Palm Beach, Florida. Two years earlier, his whole life had been changed by success guru Anthony Robbins at a motivational seminar. Before that, John did not remember much about his early twenties other than that those years involved plenty of drugs, alcohol, and fights.

John was on his way to Hawaii for another weeklong seminar with his savior Anthony Robbins. He patiently explained that he thought the Bible was fine, but he did not think it applied to life today. Robbins, he said quite confidently, was like a new messiah whose teachings would change the face of the world. High over the Mississippi River, across the panhandle of Texas, and into the Los Angeles airport, John spoke with passion about the new life he had discovered thanks to Anthony Robbins. At the airport, he handed me his business card, and we parted as new friends. His conversation had, indeed, made time pass quickly, and yet he left me off-balance.

How is it that a motivational speaker can cause such a profound life change? Meanwhile, some of us who profess faith in the Lord of the universe find ourselves caught in stagnant lives that at times seem very uninspired...and very uninspiring. How does my own life give witness to the greatness of *my* Savior? Later that same day, we went strolling down Hollywood Boulevard with our daughter and son-in-law. We happened to pass a pay phone where a young man shouted angrily into the receiver, "Don't you see? You're just making sure my music don't get no airtime on the radio!" If we want Christ to get more "airtime" in this world, other people will have to see at least the same level of commitment in us that I found in a carpet layer from West Palm Beach.

Blessings

Blessings are laced through Scripture like bright ribbons. Beginning with the first chapter of Genesis, God blesses his creation. In the final chapter of the Book of Revelation, God pronounces even more blessings as he waits for us in the world to come.

Not only are we blessed, we are able to be blessings to one another. Years ago on a hot summer evening, our son Chris sat with us watching a TV show about miracles and angels. That in itself was a minor miracle because, at age seventeen, he was usually at work or out with his friends. Sharing his company made a nice moment. It might have ended there, but it didn't.

The morning after that television show, I (Ann) decided to make a trip to a library near downtown. Chris decided to go along. We stayed for an hour or so, checked out some books, and started to leave. Near the door, we were stopped by a young mother with a baby in her arms. It was more than 95 degrees outside, and she was worried that her dilapidated stroller would not provide enough shade for her baby. Could we give them a ride home?

We were glad to be able to help. We did not say much as we drove. She and the baby had come many blocks in the heat. After we had gone a couple of miles, we dropped her in front of her house. I wondered how my son felt about our good deed. For a few minutes after we drove on, Chris said nothing. Then he said quietly, "Mom, we were the angels." I congratulated myself for seizing the opportunity to show my son how to put faith into action. Too often we Christians have a way of patting ourselves on the back for too little effort. We both felt pretty good about ourselves, and that seemed to be the end of it.

Recently, I mentioned that small good deed from long ago to a friend. She reminded me that we are the ones who are most blessed by those whom we are privileged to serve. I realized that we most certainly had been blessed by the young mother's presence and by the opportunity to help her and her baby.

Soon thereafter, I recalled a conversation with Chris, who is now grown, married, and living in another state. He prepared long and hard for his job in technology. That is why we were surprised when he said something was missing in his work. He said he just did not feel as though what he did was making a difference in anybody's life. He could not put his finger on it, but he felt that he needed to do something more meaningful, perhaps even in another field. I struggled to find a way to make the connection between what he was saying and where I thought he wanted to go. Then, thinking back, I asked him if he remembered the day we gave the mother and baby a ride home from the library. He said he did. I asked if he was missing the feeling he had when we helped them. After a long pause he answered, "Yes."

Who was most blessed? We were able to save a young mother a few steps. In return, she ignited a pilot light in our son's heart.

Funnel Cakes

A few years ago, Grandma Smith cut a recipe for funnel cakes out of the paper and brought it to us. We thanked her and made a mental note to give it a try one Sunday afternoon. What we did not tell her was that, in a sense, our family was already experienced at making our own "funnel cakes." However, the funnel cakes we made rarely had anything to do with eating.

It all started some fifteen years ago when Grandpa Smith moved to Indiana and tasted his first funnel cake at a street festival. Not only was he instantly in love with the taste, Grandpa immediately envisioned instant wealth. He began talking about buying a mobile booth and some cooking equipment. Using the trailer hitch he already had on the back of his car, we were going to pull that booth from festival to festival all over the country and amass a funnel-cake fortune in no time.

Actually, his line of thinking was nothing new. Being a family of meager means, for many years we have been seized with visions guaranteed to put all of us on easy street. It takes little more than a vacant lot or empty building to inspire us with dreams of a cozy diner, an herb store, or gift shop perfect for that location. We had our own moneymaking versions of worm farms, mink ranches, and beekeeping long before such things became fashionable.

Soon after Grandpa discovered the funnel cake business, the term took on a whole new meaning in our household. Even today, when one of us begins talking about owning a bed and breakfast, fixing up a storefront, or building a log house, another family member brings that person back to reality by asking, "Are we making funnel cakes again?" Yet there is an important dimension to all of our hypothetical "funnel-caking" business ventures: our dreams always include working beside our children, ensuring success and wealth for all of us. In a sense, we think God himself might have had something similar in mind when he created this world. The art and business of developing something that is good, beautiful, and new is joyful work. Sharing the work of creation along with beloved children is joy multiplied both for God and for parents.

In Praise of Old Cars

Blessed are those who understand the value of an old car. When our first child went to college in 1986, we bought an almost-new "pre-owned" car. Today, that same car, with almost 130,000 miles on it, still sits in our driveway. It has served us well for over a dozen years through our children's three college degrees and three weddings. In our family, we refer to this old car as "The Bonnie."

The poor thing truly has seen better days. The soft-top roof gave up and split down the middle years ago. At first, this did not look too bad. Before we ever got around to fixing it with a piece of duct tape, the gap widened into something resembling the Panama Canal. Over the years, this allowed little leaks to develop in odd places, like the top of the back window. We had a pink hospital tub sitting in the back window to catch the runoff and prevent it from pooling in the right-hand side of the floor. This turned out to be a blessing in disguise because it helped to keep our memories sharp. When we heard a rainstorm in the middle of the night, we learned to remember to empty the pink tub before we took off the next morning. Otherwise, the first time we hit the brakes, a minor tidal wave engulfed anyone sitting in the path of the tub. All except one of the power windows failed, and the air-conditioning became a vague memory. That was not bad in the winter, but in the summer Bonnie became the "penance mobile." Whatever sins we committed must surely have been forgiven in proportion to the number of miles driven in August.

The problem was, in spite of her appearance and advanced years, Bonnie continued to serve us faithfully. Even with temperatures well-below freezing, a turn of the key would start the ignition in less than thirty seconds. Also, in January, water in the pink tub froze overnight so that we did not have to remember to empty it.

Lately, we have come to realize that Bonnie probably will not make it through another winter. She has been both a blessing and a lesson for our family. A good, strong, faithful heart on the inside is a far more precious gift than a sleek body.

Starving to Death

Our daughter sat doing her homework at the kitchen table. She had turned on the TV to provide the necessary background needed to solve complex math problems. Suddenly, something caught her attention and she called us to come and see. People were performing amazing acts to get themselves into the *Guinness Book of World Records*. Two beefy-looking guys tried to outdo each other to set a world record for blowing up hot water bottles until they exploded. If this was not amazing enough, a few minutes later a muscular, often-divorced father of twelve stretched himself out on the pavement and invited several eighteen-wheel trucks to drive over his midsection. After the man survived this feat, the announcer applauded him for his bravery and courage. We wondered what record the man was trying to break. We also wondered if an ex-wife might have volunteered to drive one of the trucks!

For the past few years, the hottest shows on television have tried to top one another with material guaranteed to numb whatever brain cells we have left. Fortunately, our family does not get caught up watching a group of strangers on a deserted island back-stab themselves to wealth. We also have not been attracted to watching housefuls of people pick one another into oblivion for a monetary reward. The problem may be that we know of too many examples in real life where this kind of behavior already happens. The point is that entertainment has become more like a carnival sideshow than a way to rejuvenate our overburdened minds. Consequently, we often end up feeling like voyeurs: fascinated, but embarrassed by our own poor taste.

Some time ago, we saw a show about comedians from the early days of television. Sid Caesar, Red Skelton, George Burns, and Gracie Allen surprised us with the freshness of their comedy.

It felt good to laugh again at clever humor not done at the expense of others. Our minds no longer seem facile enough to create comedy capable of surprise and delight. What has happened to our culture over a few short years? We can only conclude that how we entertain ourselves is a reflection of our society as a whole. The way we feed our minds matches the way we feed our bodies. We refine the nutrients out of our food and consume more volume with poorer nutrition. We have the bodies to prove it. Much of what passes for entertainment is also volume without substance. It feeds neither our intellect nor our soul. We are overstuffed with mental junk food consumed in the name of entertainment. Physically, spiritually, and mentally, all of us may be slowly starving to death in the middle of abundance.

Yellow Buses

This morning I (Ann) drove to work behind a yellow school bus. At each of several stops, children climbed on board. Some, urged on by mothers waving from the door, came dragging their feet. Most looked as though they would rather be back in their beds. A few jumped up and down. One waved his arms like a bird and appeared glad to be swallowed up into the world of school.

I was struck by how little school buses have changed since the early 1950s when I waited at the end of a country lane outside of Charleston, South Carolina. In those days, the talk at the bus stop was of the war in Korea. On frosty mornings, the high-school boys spoke about whose brother or cousin had been "called up" or who might be the next in line to go.

One spring afternoon, a six-foot rattlesnake trying to cross a lonesome stretch of road fell victim to the wheels of our bus. The driver dared not climb out to see if it had been killed. As we all craned our necks to see, she backed the bus over the snake a couple of times just for good measure.

There were bus rides home with report cards we could hardly wait to share and some rides where we tried to think of ways to get rid of it before our stop. Maybe the report card could just fall beneath the seat and stay there among the empty lunch sacks and gum wrappers.

There were bus rides for field trips along with the anxiety about who would be my seatmate. Would the teacher assign me to sit next to the new kid or, perhaps, someone I did not like? Those trips often included a stop at the beach. Gritty sand and the smell of suntan lotion bonded us into community on the ride home.

Once my brother and I could not make it home from the grocery store in time to board the church bus for a trip. That bus had an accident in which no one was seriously injured. While my brother and I were sorry we had missed out on the excitement, Mom saw God's hand at work protecting us.

Major life themes are played out on school buses. What can a small body do when the bully sits in the seat behind and pulls her hair every day? Does she tell on him, just endure it, or turn around and punch him hard in the nose—never mind the consequences—just to see the shocked look on his face? Do we choose to sit beside the girl nobody likes, or just let her suffer alone, her face pressed to the window pretending it does not matter? Tragedies are carried out on school buses, but so are triumphs.

The road to Emmaus is a passage between the life we leave behind and the new life we hope to embrace. This in-between time offers opportunities for decisions. While the resurrection is the event that defines our lives, it is important to remember that the character we take into the new life is formed as we journey along the road on the way home.

7

Ordinary Time

For everything there is a season, and a time for every matter under heaven.

ECCLESIASTES 3:1

Opportunity Knocks (Softly)

At dinner with friends one Sunday evening, the conversation turned to missed opportunities. All of us had a few lingering regrets over opportunities we had missed because of our own lack of vision. For instance, during the summer of 1965 in San Francisco, friends invited Jim to go with them to hear Arthur Fiedler and the Boston Pops give a free concert in Golden Gate Park. He stayed in the dorm to prepare a class presentation due the next day. For months his friends talked about how wonderful the music had been and what a great time they had had. Jim cannot recall anything about his presentation, but he does think of his lost opportunity every time we watch the Boston Pops on television.

I made similar regrettable decisions at various points in my life. While in Massachusetts for a few months, a friend invited me to go with her to hear Robert Frost read some of his poetry. I refused because I had to study for a test the next day. I cannot remember anything about the test, but I bet my friend still remembers Robert Frost. A year or so later, my roommate begged me to go with her to hear a wonderful cellist give a free concert. Since I had never heard of Pablo Casals, I politely declined. A few years later in Baltimore, I saw a sign in front of a museum inviting the public to come in and meet an artist. I wandered into an exhibit of Andrew Wyeth's paintings. The art was breathtaking. He had such genius for painting real people in ordinary circumstances. The line to buy a print and have the artist sign it was long, and besides, at $50 a print, who could have afforded it? I wandered out empty-handed.

All of us have some small "if only" moments. What about the great-grandfather who went out West to prospect for gold? He split up with his partner two days before the other man struck it rich. Then there was a woman in Louisiana who many, many years ago turned down a date with a young naval officer by the name of John F. Kennedy.

The problem with golden opportunities is that they often arrive disguised in ordinary moments. The challenge for us is to seize the opportunities presented by ordinary moments and to say "yes" to life. By doing so, we open ourselves to such positive results as the blind date that becomes the love of our life, the gift of satisfying work, opportunities for our children, and wonderful experiences with great friends. Saying "yes" to life gives the Spirit room to work. Now that we understand how easy it is to miss opportunities, we become more determined to embrace small moments. In doing so, we might stumble into the company of a great poet, hear music by a master, or end up with a Wyeth print hanging on the living room wall.

Notes From the Floor

As we write between Memorial Day and the anniversary of D-Day, we find ourselves sorting out what is important in our lives and what is not. A couple of days ago while cleaning out old files, we came across a folder labeled "Notes From the Floor." Years ago as a teacher in a seventh-grade classroom, I (Ann) sometimes found notes left behind by students. I collected those notes in this folder while telling the students someday they would see their work published in a book that would make all of us rich and famous.

Reading through this folder, I see once again a room full of students burning with adolescent energy and angst. One note declares simply, "The life of SLAVES!" Most of the notes fret over friendships in jeopardy and reflect the adolescent struggle to stay connected in a sometimes hostile teenage culture. One is a handwritten "Hail Mary" while another note threatens, "If you ever want to see your workbook again, meet me at 3 PM tonight." There are desperate pleas for homework answers and much speculation about Michael Jordan and the Chicago Bulls' chances in the NBA finals. Those were the days of Desert Storm, and some of my students had friends and family headed for the conflict in Iraq. The anxiety in some of the notes is a reflection of those anxious times.

On Memorial Day evening, we read through the notes while we watched a program called "War Letters" on our local PBS channel. Letters sent home from men in the Revolutionary War through the Civil War, World Wars I and II, Korea, Vietnam, and Desert Storm were read aloud against a backdrop of war footage. Though the letters read were from wars spanning more than two hundred years, they echoed similar themes. Young men (and women, in the later wars) caught in the worst of conflicts longed for warm, dry beds and the simple pleasure of hot food shared in the company of family and friends. They wearied of fighting, destruction, and death. Often they promised to be home soon, a promise many of them would not be able to keep. For some, these letters were their last words home before dying in battle.

While reading through the folder of classroom notes, we realized some of those same young teens writing notes back in the days of Desert Storm are probably serving in Iraq today. They may have gone from being writers of classroom notes to writing their own chapter of war letters home. No doubt their letters, too, will reveal the fragile humanity common to all of us. Wisdom 11:22 reminds us that, in God's sight, the whole world is nothing more than a grain of dust or a drop of morning dew. In the end, the classroom notes and the latest war letters home remind us that our ultimate longings revolve around the simple things of life: a warm, dry bed, enough to eat, and someone to love who will love us back.

Last One in the Berry Patch

In spite of many things to do this morning, I (Ann) am driving to the U-Pick strawberry patch. This has been a very poor season for strawberries. It is probably too late in the picking season for the patch to still be open. We have had rain for the past several days, and it looks as though it will start again any minute. As if all of this is not enough, it is unseasonably chilly and a sharp wind is blowing. All of these things fit this day very well. Let me explain.

We have had kids in high school for the past nineteen years, more or less. Things have certainly changed. Our older son graduated from high school and left for college fifteen years ago. We reassured ourselves by saying that in four years he would come home to work. That never happened. When our older daughter left for college, we planned for her to return, marry a local young man, and have grandchildren in a house nearby. After she moved to California, we thought we might have better luck with our second son. After all, his wife's family lives only a few hours from us. Our younger son and his wife now live in another state. By now, we know what the odds are that any of our children are going to fulfill our fantasies. With our youngest, Laura, we have no illusions. Children come into our lives for a few years, and then they carry our hearts away with them. On this weekend, Laura will graduate from high school. That is the real reason that this is a perfect morning to seek refuge in a cold, wet berry patch.

The field is on top of a hill, and the rows face west, making it all the easier to catch the full force of this sharp wind. There are three or four other pickers out gleaning the bushes. As one couple is leaving, the husband walks toward me shaking his head. "Nothing left out here," he shouts, "It's all gone!" I don't care. I believe berries are here, hiding under leaves, and they are not safe from me this morning. Defiant, I claim a row. After a few minutes, the teenage girl in charge of the patch yells over to me, "I'm going to have you move to one of these rows beyond me." I am in no mood to be helped. "OK," I tell her, "but I've found berries right here. Don't go sending me to where you don't have any berries." She backs down. I stay put.

The ground is saturated, and the few other pickers are bending over or squatting along the rows. That is no way to make progress in a berry patch. I am wearing a short-sleeved shirt and jeans. Crawling on all fours, the knees of my jeans get soaked right through. The wind raises goose bumps on my arms. This is wonderful. My parents were from the old school. They believed anything we did should be done right. Even misery.

The only berries left are the ones down under the leaves and straw. Not many people bother with berries this small. While I am picking, I am thinking about all of our kids and the years of love, sunshine, and pure energy they have poured into our lives. It takes me an hour to pick about nine pounds of berries. When I finally stand up, there is no one else left in the field. Even the girl in charge is gone. Leaving the field to pay for the berries, I cannot help but think. Seems this is the way life is: You crawl along, picking all the fruit you can find, until one day you straighten up, look around, and realize that you are the only one left in the berry patch.

Loved Into Being

Parenthood may be the most dangerous adventure any of us ever undertake. We know wonderful young adults who have come out of terrible homes. We also know devout, spirit-filled parents with children who cause them much pain. Everybody has ideas on how to bring up children. Sometimes it does seem that those without children often feel they are the greatest experts.

For instance, before our eldest child Jim came along, we knew exactly what kind of parents we intended to be. We planned to be potters and shape the "clay" we had been given into a wonderful adult. Instead, we quickly realized that, when it came to parenting, we were big time fumblers. No matter. Young Jim seemed interested only in how things worked. He wanted to know about science—only science. If it didn't involve science, it didn't matter. When he began to toddle, I learned to listen for the quiet. If things got too quiet, I ran to find out what he was up to. One day I went to another room while he rearranged the pots and pans in the kitchen. By the time I returned, he proudly displayed all of the canned goods, arranged by size with labels removed. We had surprise suppers for a month.

Who was this child and where did he come from? Instead of being potters, we were more like gardeners with a mystery plant and no instructions. We ran along behind him while he consumed one branch of science after another. We sat in the museum while he took classes in astronomy. His dad helped him launch model rockets while I prayed until they came home with their fingers intact. In junior high, he put a simple computer together from a kit. We took care of the burn when he absent-mindedly stuck his soldering iron instead of a pencil behind his ear. A favorite high-school teacher spent one summer helping him get a ham radio license. When he got a chemistry set for Christmas, we held our breath through his experiments and tried to stay calm when he announced that something had "slightly caught fire." The word we most dreaded to hear coming from his room was "oops." Today, happily, he works for a company that does scientific testing.

Our oldest son did not get great parenting from us. We had absolutely no idea how to be parents. He did get all of our love and unending years of our prayers. In return, he taught us the truest thing about parenting. All children are mysterious, exciting, joyful gifts, meant to be nurtured, loved, and treasured. When asked her secret, one elderly woman who had mothered many successful, talented children replied that she "kept pouring love in until it spilled out of them." We would like to add that even after our children are adults, we keep pouring in the love and praying that God will somehow correct all the mistakes we only now understand that we made.

When we were expecting our third child, young Jim's first-grade teacher called to tell us about an exchange she had overheard between Jim and his classmate. His playmate had asked him if he knew how babies were born. Our son replied, "God loves them into being." Though not scientific, his answer was an absolute truth. God loves all of us into being. Sometimes all we can do is love our children—to try to love them into being the kind of people God intends them to be.

Did Somebody Yell "Timber"?

Last week the tree cutter came to our street. He chopped down an unwanted hackberry tree growing next to the fence, a large bush that had migrated from the yard next door, and our basketball goal post. The chain saw did its work, and in less than twenty minutes the tree and bush were gone. The goal post next to the driveway came down even faster, taking years of memories away with it.

In the past couple of weeks, other trees we have not wanted to lose have been brought down. Several large trees around town blew down in a storm a few nights ago. Green and strong, the thick trunks snapped off midway like broken kindling. All of this worries us because sometimes we resemble trees. With our roots sunk firmly in the earth and our days spent offering shade to those who come beneath our branches, we wrap ourselves in a measure of dignity. Then life, swinging an axe, strides among our company without any regard for even the sturdiest among us. All of us are vulnerable to unexpected blows.

Recently, a friend who had provided a service for an organization for the past fifteen years was told he was no longer needed. (*Whack! Let's give this one a ringing blow. Don't chop it down all the way. Just give it a good gash or two.*) In this same week a friend known for her grace, intelligence, and goodness learned she has an inoperable cancer. (*Thump! We'll leave this one half-standing for now.*) Finally, our friend Gilbert decided to spend a few extra minutes outside in his garden on a Saturday afternoon. His wife of sixty years looked for him a little while later and found him where he had suddenly died. With one blow our community lost a mighty, seasoned oak.

The farther we go up the mountain, the thinner the forest. Sometimes we take a deep breath, spread our branches wider, and savor all that life has to offer. Other times, we wonder why we have been left standing and we try to figure out what we are supposed to be doing. Meanwhile, the sound of the axe striking so close causes us to tremble and reflect.

Door Dings

Last Saturday morning, I (Ann) pulled into a parking space at the shopping center. In a hurry to buy some envelopes and get to the post office, I threw open the car door. This was followed by the sound of metal striking against metal. The car next to me had been on the receiving end of a "door ding," and I was the perpetrator.

The owner of the car happened to be a woman young enough to be my daughter. She was a pleasant person, well brought up and a credit to her parents. She calmly pointed out the nicked paint on the front fender and, without raising her voice, said firmly, "Ma'am, I'm going to have to ask you to pay for that...." Of course she was right. We have always encouraged our own children to own up to their mistakes. The cost of my quick trip to the post office had just escalated to something in the neighborhood of a few hundred dollars.

Now, here is the part where new brides will want to pay attention. The worst thing about a door ding is not what it is going to cost. The worst part is having to go home and tell your husband about the stupid thing you have just done. After more than thirty-five years of marriage, there have been many "door dings" in our lives. Over the years, we have developed a finely tuned system for breaking this kind of news, and I am going to tell you how this works.

That Saturday morning I waited until Jim came in and settled himself comfortably in his favorite chair across from me. Then, I casually began with a litany of our blessings: "You know, we've come this far in life and we are so fortunate neither of us has a serious health problem." (*Pause here so that both of you can appreciate this magnificent gift.*) I continued with, "All of the kids are doing well right now. Isn't that great? Katie is coming home, and you've got vacation coming. Won't that be fun?" By now he had a sense of where this was going, and he asked cautiously, "Which one of the kids called?" "None of them," I reassured him. There was a long pause between us before I raised my hand slightly and added, "But there is one little problem." In a casual, offhand tone, I relayed the news about the door ding. However, in light of how overwhelmed we were with blessings, this was very small news indeed.

For all the young women out there who are about to embark on marriage, this is how to handle such situations. After all, life is full of door dings, especially when two people travel together side by side. We take so much for granted. As a deacon friend of ours once said, "God gives us enough to keep us going." Given the many great blessings that surround us, how else can we approach the minor dings in life but with gratitude?

The Look

Somewhere we have read that most of the communication that passes between husband and wife is nonverbal. That seems truer for us the longer we are together. Recently we gave some thought to this type of communication, and we decided that it all boils down to a "look." We read each other's hearts and emotions on our faces. Actually, there is a repertoire of several looks, each capable of conveying volumes without a word being spoken. There is the look that says "Let's get out of here" if we are both bone-tired and sitting somewhere other than in our own home at the end of the day. Another look useful in large gatherings says, "Did you catch it? Wasn't that funny?" Then there is the one look above all others that is the loaded weapon. This one can be deadly even across a crowded room. It says, "Now you've said something that goes too far and one of us is in trouble here." Most schoolteachers have developed this last one to a fine art for classroom use.

Nonverbal communication happens when we get to know one another reasonably well. It reduces communication to a shorthand that is often more truthful and significant than words. In the Book of Leviticus, even God is described as telling the Israelites he would "set his face against them" if they broke his laws. In fact, in Scripture God often sets his face against those who care too little for what is right. Just as God hides his face from those who do wrong, he also makes his face shine on those who make the effort to honor his laws.

Does God still communicate with us nonverbally? In moments of sin, the pain in our conscience feels a great deal like the pain we once felt when our parents gave us the "look" that meant we had done something wrong or gone too far. At other times, in moments when we have lived our faith well, there is an inner glow from the Spirit. That feeling is something akin to the way we felt when we hit a home run or scored a goal and caught a glimpse of a parent's face in the stands. The metaphors of God "setting his face against us," or making his face to "shine upon us," are beautiful expressions of the intimacy we share with God. In the best of relationships, there are times when words are not needed. In moments when meaning must be communicated quickly and with truth, one look says it all.

What's It Worth?

After supper on Monday evenings, Grandma and I (Ann) liked to stay at the kitchen table to watch the *Antiques Roadshow*. We were amazed by how much some of the items on display were worth. A lamp that is uglier than some of the ones we happen to own is worth $60,000. A vase somebody bought from a farmer for $15 is actually worth $25,000! "Sure it's worth $25,000," Grandma pointed out, "but where are they going to find the one person actually willing to pay that much for it?" We often agreed that some of those things did seem a bit overpriced.

Grandma and I had been saving stuff for years. She once mentioned something about a small brass gong on her dresser. Somebody brought it back from India as a gift for Great-Grandma Wilson. We both believed that anything old and foreign ought to be worth a lot of money. I wondered about the artifacts Jim and I brought home from Africa. Then, too, there is my tin full of bicentennial quarters tucked in a certain dresser drawer. One day in the distant future, our heirs might turn up on the *Antiques Roadshow* clutching something we have squirreled away. They will gratefully learn that what they have is worth a bunch of money, and we will be vindicated for holding on to certain things.

While Grandma and I were talking, we remembered Great-Grandma Moore's bedspread. In 1939, my great-grandmother used a few pennies to buy a ball of string. She used this to crochet some circles. Then she bought more string and crocheted more circles, and, finally, she crocheted all of those circles together. After hundreds of hours and thousands of small stitches, she presented my father and mother with her handmade bedspread as a wedding gift.

Though I remembered seeing this spread several times while I grew up, neither my mother nor I knew where it might be. Part of the problem with being savers is that we knew we had almost everything; it's just that we always had a hard time locating specific things. A few weeks later, this precious spread did turn up in one of our own closets at home. The thing I treasure most about this spread is the love behind the gift. No matter where we moved, I knew I had a great-grandmother who loved us so much she could take common string and, with patience and work, create something of lasting beauty for us to keep.

Some of the things that turn up on the *Antiques Roadshow* have stories like this connected to them. Others, though they may be worth thousands of dollars, have no deeper meaning attached to them. What gives a thing value? The cross of our faith was something plain, no different than thousands of crosses used in that time. The immense love and sacrifice attached to the cross gave meaning to it so that it became something of immeasurable worth to each of us. It is good for all of us to reflect on what it is in our own lives that truly have value and what things are simply objects that, in the end, lack any meaningful worth.

Can't Hurt, Might Help

I (Ann) wasn't paying much attention to the conversation going on between the grocery cashier and the teenage girl busy bagging my groceries. "Would that make a difference to you?" she asked, and then I realized her question was directed to me. Seeing I did not have a clue about what she meant, the girl repeated her question, "If your daughter did something that made you really, really hate her and she sent you flowers with a bunch of cute notes, would that make a difference?"

What an odd question. There are many things that cannot be

explained in a grocery checkout line, and this easily fell into that category. First of all, very few parents really, really hate their children…ever. Parents can get furious with children, at times, but even then, hate is not part of the picture. The opposite of love is indifference, not fury. Parents can occasionally get really angry with children who behave in ways unworthy of the piece of God's glory we know them to be, but we are never indifferent.

The girl had stopped bagging my groceries. Obviously, her question was not rhetorical. Her absolutely beautiful, innocent face reminded me of our children and the times we mended rips in our own family life. Mental images came back of little bunches of weeds or wildflowers offered by grubby hands and of a child offering to do extra chores in penance. Somewhere we still have a wrinkled, tear-stained note scrawled by our then-seven-year-old daughter Katie. The apology reads simply, "I am Dubble Sad."

This teenage girl waiting for an answer in such a public place could not possibly know how many parents go around with a load of forgiveness walled up inside, just hoping for some small opening to let it pour out. The parable of the prodigal son strikes at the heart of families on every continent. All over the world, in every age, parents have longed for a chance to welcome a child home. How many parents today would welcome the opportunity to pour out forgiveness on a child?

Last week we had a parish reconciliation service. A few of the children were celebrating this sacrament for the first time. They came into the sanctuary a little apprehensive, not quite sure what to expect. After celebrating individually and as a community, the sense of quiet joy filling the sanctuary had come to rest on the children's faces.

Whatever offense this young woman in front of me had committed, I hoped she and her mother would find the peace and joy of reconciliation. Probably her poor mother wanted things fixed up even more than she did. The girl, still waiting, repeated her question: "Flowers and notes won't make it worse?" "It won't hurt, and it will probably help," I told her. "Are you sure?" she asked. "Count on it. Give her the flowers."

As indicated by the parable of the prodigal son, Jesus knew that unspent forgiveness is way too awful a burden for any poor parent to have to carry.

Keeper of the Rectory

My (Jim) childhood home was located just down the hill from our parish. Attending the parish school, my brothers and I became quite familiar with the priests who lived in the rectory on the corner. Our parents were very active parish members, and they often sent me up to the rectory on errands. In those days, as many as four priests lived in the rectory. As far as the kids were concerned, however, it was the housekeeper who had the real power. In response to the timid knock of a child sent on a mission, her imposing figure filled the doorway. One quickly learned that if you wanted to speak with Father, you had better mind your manners when you spoke with the housekeeper. Although her demeanor could be overwhelming at first, her parental warmth ultimately put us at ease. Many times I headed home with a fresh baked cookie or a piece of candy in my pocket.

Whatever happened to those women who took care of our rectories? Older, sometimes widowed, they not only cooked and cleaned; they provided our priests with a sense of home and hearth. Hidden beneath a humble appearance, some of them had more power than many realized. Sad to say, as our rectories have become emptier, such women have become scarcer. They worked in an often unrecognized yet noble profession that stretched back to the time when Mary and Martha provided hospitality for our Lord and his disciples.

Recently, Helen, one such rectory housekeeper, passed away. She died in her living room with family and priests gathered around. More people than anyone might expect turned out for the funeral of such an unpretentious woman. Five priests sat in the sanctuary. For some of them, Helen had been their house-keeper, sometimes their sister or parent, and always their friend. In the tradition of those who had gone before her, she had re-minded them that, in spite of their ordination, they were still mortal men who needed the counsel of a caring friend. In her own way, Helen was a remarkable woman. She ironed shirts at ten cents apiece to put a daughter through nursing school. One son graduated from West Point. Another son graduated from law school. A third son drowned at age sixteen, and a few years after his tragic death, she buried her husband, the love of her life. For twenty years she served as the housekeeper at a rectory where she made the priests stay out of "her" kitchen. Once, she made a blueberry pie out of the blueberries Father had been saving for his personal cereal bowl. He dared not object. Saturday nights Helen dressed up and went out dancing at the VFW. Helen loved life and she loved to dance. She told her family that she wanted them to put "Helen had a ball" on her tombstone.

In his eulogy, Father Camillus said he had told Helen that he planned to dance along with her in heaven. He recalled others by name who had served in our rectories. At the end, he added Helen's name to the list of faithful housekeepers who are no longer with us. Like Mary and Martha, a rectory housekeeper's work is based on service. Helen had mastered the art of serving those who in turn serve our spiritual needs. Helen's life was a memorial to the powerful strength found in simple service.

Closing the Circle

Once Jim and I attended a large charity event to honor and support the work of the Little Sisters of the Poor. Though it was a lavish affair, almost everything had been donated. No one wanted to miss an opportunity to give something back to the good sisters. I sat next to a friend who happens to lead a rich and interesting life, and she had a wonderful story to tell. It was a story of simple events that intertwined into quite a remarkable tale.

In the 1930s, her mother and father had built a home in what was once a fashionable neighborhood. They referred to it as "The House of Seven Gables." That was where she and her older half brother grew up. After her mother passed away in 1951, her father lived in the house alone for a while. Later, he went to live at the home run by the Little Sisters of the Poor. When he died in 1985, she and her half brother sold the house through a realtor. They never met the new owners, and the story might have ended there.

One day not long ago, her brother happened to see their old family home for sale by the owner in the paper. Out of curiosity, he called the number listed. The same woman who had bought the house years ago answered the phone. She was glad to hear from him. The house had been a happy place for her, and she had a question for him: Had their mother ever lost anything in the house? He replied that mother had lost her wedding ring in 1941. The owner said, "I have your mother's ring." The woman and her husband remodeled the kitchen after they moved into the house in 1985. In the course of the remodeling, the plumber found the ring in the drain and had given it to her. That ring had been stuck in the drain for forty-four years. The woman had kept it safe for another twenty years. Through the integrity of the plumber and the woman, after sixty-four years the lost ring finally made its way back into my friend's family.

That night, close to seven hundred people came together to celebrate the gift among us of the Little Sisters of the Poor. Since 1882, the Little Sisters have cared for, loved, and kept safe the aging mothers, fathers, aunts, uncles, and grandparents of our community. That night, our community completed the circle. Love always comes home.

A Nielsen Family

Some time ago while Grandma Smith was still with us, we got a call at the dinner hour. As soon as we heard a friendly voice mispronounce our name and ask how we were that "fine evening," we braced ourselves for a pitch for storm windows, aluminum siding, or a cemetery plot. Instead, this caller invited us to be a "Nielsen family" for one week.

Our hearts skipped. An official organization finally wanted to know our opinion about what is being shown on television! We gladly accepted this opportunity to upgrade the quality of American life. We failed to mention that we have never bothered to get cable or a satellite dish, thus eliminating any votes for the Home Shopping Network, MTV, or HBO. We also left out the fact that Grandma had difficulty following the plot of many shows due to her very poor hearing. Mostly, we sat with her to watch the *Antiques Roadshow* and *Wheel of Fortune*, both of which could be followed without actually hearing much of anything.

Within a week or so, we received four journals, one for each television in the house. In front of each of our journals, they had allotted fifty-four spaces to fill in all the channels we use. Three of our four sets have rabbit ears and one is hooked up to the only rooftop antenna left in the neighborhood. We listed seven channels, five of which are clear in good weather. By the time the Nielsen Company realized with whom they were dealing, we felt certain they would allot our journals to a special bin.

We quickly became mindful of the programming that we watched. We had tuned in to one of those mindless sitcoms when we suddenly remembered our heavy responsibility as a Nielsen family. Quickly we switched to *Great Museums of the World* on PBS. Being a Nielsen family gave us a sense of power and led to a discussion on how we might maximize our influence. If something particularly distasteful came on, we could switch channels to an opposing show just to pump up the opposition's ratings. We wondered if it counted if the TV was on with Grandma asleep in her chair in front of it. For that matter, did they have a category for shows all of us have slept through? Our week as a Nielsen family ended far too soon, and once again we were among the powerless.

Our week as a Nielsen family led us to seriously reflect on the quality of programming that we watched. It also led us to a far more important question regarding the quality of the example we set by our own Christian lives: As followers of Christ, are we a show worth watching?

Above the Treetops

We went for a walk early last Saturday morning. Near the top of a hill, with the city spread out asleep beneath us, we watched a hot air balloon rise in silence above the trees. Within a few minutes, a second balloon followed. Someone once told us that the people inside the basket never feel a breeze because the balloon always travels at the same speed as the wind. While the sun rose behind the balloons, I wondered about the people in the fragile basket. Who would do such a thing? How can they just let go of everything and float away like that? I envied them, just a little bit. It wasn't the ride I envied; I like keeping my feet on the ground. I envied the detachment of the riders.

We all have illusions that make it possible for us to keep our feet on the ground. Our homes will always be waiting. Children will come home safely. Our jobs will be there tomorrow. Our spouse will stay healthy. Priests will be available when we need them. Sooner or later, a crisis comes along to shatter our illusions. Other times, life just eats away at our illusions, leaving us to wonder what happened. Sometimes the only way to deal with broken illusions is to let go and drift above them to get a different perspective.

Throughout Scripture, God challenges some of his most useful people with crises big enough to shatter illusions. Often these people have to decide whether or not they can let go of what, in the past, gave them comfort and security. Much of Scripture is about people who could or could not let go. Noah let go and rested totally dependent on the grace of God to bring him and his family safely back to dry ground. Abraham had to let go and become a wanderer before God could turn him into the father of God's Chosen People. The Israelites had to let go of the familiarity and security of Egypt before they could make their way to the Promised Land. On the other hand, the people who decided to build the tower of Babel could not let go, and neither could Lot's wife. Even though his own debt had been forgiven, the unforgiving servant in Matthew's Gospel (18:21–35) could not let go and forgive the debt of others. Sometimes letting go has nothing to do with possessions. It is more about letting go of wrongs and pain. For example, in the Hebrew Scriptures Joseph forgave his brothers of the wrongs they committed against him and saved his family.

Christ himself won more than one battle to stay detached

from this earth. Satan used the illusions of power, wealth, and plenty to try to tie Christ to this world and convince him to abandon his mission. Even near the end of this mission in the Garden of Gethsemane, Christ struggled to hand his will over to the Father, proving to the rest of us that letting go is a lifelong process. Or, as author Rick Warren says in *The Purpose Driven Life*, "The trouble with a living sacrifice is that it can always crawl off the altar." Part of the life of faith is to continue the struggle to let go, stay in the basket, and let the wind of the Spirit take us where it will.

Say Nothing

"How great a forest is set ablaze by a small fire! And the tongue is a fire" (James 3:5–6).

As far as our tongues being able to ignite a fire, nothing has changed in the last two thousand years. That is why we appreciate the virtue of often saying nothing when it comes to dealing with our adult children. Over the years, we have had plenty of opportunity to practice keeping quiet, even though much wonderful wisdom has frequently been screaming to come out of our brains.

Our practice in the art of saying nothing began when our oldest was nine or ten. One night young Jim decided to make supper for all of us. This was the kind of behavior we liked to encourage. After a couple of hours of some pot banging and small appliance noises, he summoned us to the table. The featured dish turned out to be a large bowl of blue mashed potatoes. Not powder blue. These were a brilliant aquamarine blue. Seems he thought plain white mashed potatoes were, well, dull. Blue food would be more interesting. We agreed. God gave us the grace to quietly consume the blue potatoes. The fact that the food coloring dyed our mouths and made us resemble Mama and Papa Smurf for the next couple of days was a side benefit.

The other day, Ann and a friend were talking about the value of holding their tongues when things get interesting with adult children. The friend had tried to help an adult son finish filling out graduate school applications. They were in a car speeding to the airport at the time. Her husband and son were in the front seat. She sat in the back with his laptop and tried to make sense of his handwritten notes in the margins of the applications. She wanted to offer a few well-chosen thoughts about organization and the folly of leaving things until the last minute. Instead, smart woman that she is, she said nothing. Oprah has done whole shows on adult children whose lives have been turned upside-down by parents who said too much at the wrong time.

We could save our children much time and trouble in life if they only welcomed our advice. Why don't we speak up? Maybe we stay quiet because our own parents had both the kindness and confidence to remain silent and let us steer our own ship. Knowing when to say nothing may be one of the most powerful skills a parent can cultivate.

In our own relationship with the Lord, we have experienced times of silence. God says little to us and our prayers seem to go unanswered. An old German proverb says that it is always dark at the foot of the lighthouse. Could it be that God, in his infinite wisdom, sometimes "says nothing" so that we can learn the lessons that he knows we need to learn?

Peaches and Dreams

The other day I (Jim) drove a ninety-eight-year-old friend to the pharmacy. Since I had to get back to the office to finish some work, we stopped at a drive-through pharmacy window. Instead of instant service, the young clerk handed me a pager and instructed us to return when it went off. So much for fast, drive-through service. We had no place to go, so we pulled into a parking lot to wait. My friend has a surprisingly quick mind for a man born when Teddy Roosevelt was president, and on this day he felt like talking.

The recent hot, dry weather led us to reminiscing about what we did before we had air conditioning. He lived on a small farm and enjoyed picking and eating fresh fruit on hot summer days. He described filling his hat with apples and peaches and sitting on a bale of hay in a certain spot in the barn where he had a feast. The horse looked longingly at the fruit, so he shared a couple of green apples with him. The next day when the horse turned up sick, he told his stepfather about the apples. Fortunately, his stepfather had a local reputation as a healer of both animals and people, and soon all was well again.

While my friend reveled in childhood memories, I could almost taste and smell the sweet juice from a ripe peach running down my chin while pesky gnats fought for a sip. I shared how my brothers and I climbed an old apple tree at the end of the cornfield behind a house. We had our fill of green apples while we caught an occasional breeze wafting through the branches. With a faraway look in his eyes, my friend said, "I never imagined I'd live this long."

The shrill beep of the pager summoned us back to reality. We returned to the pharmacy window to pick up yet another refill of a modern drug. Perhaps it will buy him a little more time, though he has little concern about that. My friend still lives alone in his own house, and loneliness in itself is enough to starve a soul to death. Tastes and smells from long ago bring back sweet memories. However, in the later years of life, the food we need the most comes from ripe relationships. We must have a few of these on hand to bite into until the sweet juices run out...even on a hot day in a parking lot, waiting for a refill.

The Catechist

Catechists lead hidden lives. Behind every well-prepared catechist who walks into a classroom full of eager young faces is a husband, mother, or teenager pitching in with supper, babysitting, or even last-minute trips to buy markers, construction paper, or glue. In our household one recent morning, Jim frantically ran out of the bathroom. His shaving cream had disappeared. Obviously, he did not know that shaving cream is a wonderful cleaner for Formica tables. I had used it the day before to clean the tables for religious education! Catechists take this kind of knowledge for granted. Fortunately, we had an extra can of shaving cream in our home supply closet. Moments like this keep our marriage interesting.

Catechists are busy people. They have been known to feed their children fast food in the van between soccer practice and religious education classes. Real catechists prepare lessons on their lunch hour at work. Catechists bake cookies at midnight the day before the Advent program and rescue empty two-liter bottles out of wastebaskets for six-year-olds to turn into terrariums for Mother's Day. In their houses, empty margarine tubs, juice cans, and scraps of material wait to be given new life in craft projects. They save cardboard tubes from paper-towel rolls to make Old Testament scrolls. Catechists scour yard sales for children's games, small flowerpots, costume jewelry, and other useful items to have on hand..."just in case."

The life of a catechist is complicated, hectic, and fragile. A sick child or dead car battery can spell disaster. Catechists pray often and hard. They pray for their families, their children, and their coworkers. They pray for the bright faces that come to them each week. After they pray for everyone else, they also whisper hurried last-minute prayers for inspiration, patience, and strength for themselves.

At a recent Liturgy of the Word session for children at our parish, more then double the normal number of children appeared. Two mothers and a teen stepped in to help. That is what real catechists do. Finely tuned to the call of the Spirit, they see and understand where they are needed. Catechists ignore the practical voice in their heads telling them to say "no" while they add yet another expression of love and faith to their already busy lives. As true servants of God, they have a ready "yes" in their hearts.

Quietly they come each year, planting seeds to take children through tough times. They know they have been charged with laying the foundation for tomorrow's Church in young hearts and minds. Often catechists get little recognition, and words of thanks may be few and far between. Still, some serve for ten, fifteen, and twenty years or more out of gratitude for the grace of God in their lives. Sometimes, I like to remind our catechists that they have "stars in their crowns in heaven." Throughout the year, a word of thanks from all of us is also in order.

Incense and Flashing Lights

The world's largest censer, or "thurible," is in the Cathedral of Santiago Compostela in northwest Spain. This giant silver thurible is hoisted aloft and swung by means of a stout rope and eight able-bodied men. In the Middle Ages, weary and presumably unwashed pilgrims slept in straw on the floor of the cathedral. In an effort to freshen the air the next morning, the impressive thurible was pulled up near the rafters and swung back and forth in a fifty-meter arc. It filled the length of the cathedral with a sweeter aroma than the one left by the pilgrims.

We know about this thurible because our friends in their own travels happened to arrive at the cathedral on the very day someone had made a "pious offering" large enough to warrant a demonstration, even though it was not a holy day. Overhead, the giant silver pot swooped back and forth streaming incense and occasionally dropping hot cinders close enough to the modern-day pilgrims to make them duck.

Our own experience with incense and thuribles has been far more modest. We enjoy the scent of incense wafting gently through our worship space. It seems to underscore our prayer and lends a note of hushed reverence to our ritual. At least that is what our normal experience has been.

One weekend while on a retreat for deacons and their wives, however, we had a new and more startling experience with a thurible and incense. We were in a small, stone chapel where we have enjoyed community prayer many times. That afternoon seemed no different than any other. First, an opportunity for reconciliation had been scheduled, which was to be followed by adoration of the Blessed Sacrament and evening prayer. Some of us knelt for adoration during reconciliation. Incense billowed upward in a small fragrant stream. After a few minutes, it was announced that evening prayer would be delayed because the deacons and their wives were taking longer for reconciliation than had been expected. (Make of that what you will.) Incense continued to curl upward and drift below the fifteen-foot ceiling.

The atmosphere remained restful and quiet until, finally, we were all gathered. The murmur of prayer began and joined with the incense, which was now settling thick around the pews. The monstrance holding the Blessed Sacrament gleamed on the altar. Then, with a blast that startled us all, the smoke alarm jarred our senses and tore apart our words of comfort and praise. The alarm had been placed high on the wall out of reach. We kept praying, but with a little more speed in our words than when we had begun. The monstrance on the altar happened to be standing in the exact spot to reflect the flashing light from the smoke alarm. With every blast, blue flashes surrounded the host. By the end of prayer, windows had been opened. The alarm and the interesting blue flashes ceased.

As incense refreshes stale air, so too prayer refreshes lives that have grown stagnant. Even among the many distractions that fill our lives, we must persevere at prayer and remain focused on God's marvelous presence in our midst.

Down the Drain

The morning air is broken by the sound of chain saws. Two aging trees are being turned into firewood. One's roots tore up the driveway concrete. The other had branches soaring over the house. Old things sometimes have a way of going where they are not wanted. In our neighborhood, there are signs of aging in the trees, in the houses, and in the people.

The neighbors across the street have been good friends since we moved in more than thirty years ago. We have watched each other's children grow up and have seen all of them leave to pursue dreams in distant cities. Every morning now, Homer's wife leaves him alone at home while she runs the business they founded some years ago. Homer has been ill for some time and no longer has the strength to meet the demands of the work. With failing health, he remains alone at home. Knowing how independent these friends are, we try not to intrude. We also know them well enough to recognize when something is amiss.

A few days ago we noticed their front door had been left

ajar. When it stayed that way for some time, I (Jim) ventured a friendly, slightly nosy call: "Hi Homer. How are things going today? Doing OK over there?" There was an uncharacteristic tremor in our neighbor's reply. "Hot water heater busted. Basement's flooded," he said. I grabbed a mop and went over to help him cleanup.

Our cleanup efforts took a toll on both of us. After our valiant-but-futile attempt to fix the situation, we gave up and waited for the repairmen. Mostly we talked about our children. Two of his are working on advanced degrees at colleges in other states. The third just got a hefty pay raise. Beneath the pride in his voice was the truth of how much he missed them. "This house feels like a tomb," he said. "I think my time on this planet is just about done." Our neighbor is a devout man, and there was a touch of anticipation in his words.

Nothing in life is permanent. Sometimes unexpected events surge upon us and flood our lives with challenges we never expected. Even well-loved houses once full of life can become lonely tombs. Seasons change. All around us in autumn, flowers wither and leaves fall. We sense the ebb of nature. The younger generation sees only bare branches and forgets the strength hidden in roots. How can we explain that as our bodies diminish, our spirits become eager to surge forth again in the spring of resurrection?

The Autumn Path

With the arrival of autumn, we have finally been able to turn off the air conditioner and throw open the windows. The cool evening air brings in all the sounds of night we have kept out since last spring. Welcome change is in the air. It is a little darker when we hit the pavement for our early morning walk, but the fresh air is invigorating and well worth the effort. Neither of us misses the humidity of the last three months.

We are now past sixty. Changes we had expected as part of the aging process arrive on schedule. We try to make the best of them. We are moving a little slower, which gives us more time to enjoy some sights along the way. We don't hear as well as we once did, and this forces us to pay closer attention. Our feet hurt when we have to stand a long time, so we sit down for short breaks. We usually take such opportunities to rethink and adjust our plans for the remainder of the day. With my (Jim) diminishing hairline, we have saved money that might have gone for haircuts. And, we have to admit that we rarely pass up an opportunity for a "senior" discount.

Some changes were not anticipated. Surprisingly, our calendar seems much fuller than when we had a house full of kids. The focus has changed now from children to adult activities. Concerts, lectures, and church events are scrawled all over the calendar. No wonder we have so little time to rest.

Our roll as parents has also changed. Our three oldest children have established themselves in distant cities and our youngest child is off to college, though she still comes home for holidays and weekends. With our children no longer living at home, we have discovered that our involvement in their lives continues on a different level, one that involves the heart. When an adult son's or daughter's heart is hurting, so is ours. The days of holding them close, rubbing their backs, and sitting with them on the foot of the bed are gone. Instead, we sit on our bed clutching a phone and listen to what they are and are not saying. Now, when adult children have difficulties, we hold them close by embracing them with daily prayer.

While aging brings inevitable change to our lives, the part of us that will forever be a parent always stays the same. In some small way, being a parent gives us a window into the forever-loving heart of God.

Thank God for Possums

Recently, workmen installed a new sound system in our church. This was a cause for great rejoicing as the old system had been in terrible condition for many years. The work required opening the space under our more-than-one-hundred-year-old sanctuary. One morning the man working with the wires below the sanctuary hastily pulled himself out. As someone later said, he was white as a sheet and looked as though he had seen a ghost.

While sorting through the wires under the sanctuary, he had encountered some sort of critter. Its glassy eyes had been fixed upon him at close range. After a few moments of stark terror, the worker realized he had come face to face with a possum of enormous size. Our maintenance man helped him capture the creature in a five-gallon bucket. They covered it with a piece of plywood, and within a short time the possum was introduced to some new outdoor real estate down by the river.

Most likely, this possum had been in our church for a long time. It had often been sighted by our pastor and a few others who caught glimpses of it wandering close to the building late at night. Never having caused any trouble, no one paid much attention to what it did or where it went. That is the way of possums. They generally move slowly and keep such a low profile that no one knows much about what they actually do. They avoid the limelight and mind their own possum business.

Churches of every denomination are fortunate if they have a few "possums." These members live close to the church, but keep quietly in the background. They like to take care of business behind the scenes. People are aware of them, in fact some even recognize them as friends, but few know the details of what they are really about. "Possums" like to launder the linens for the eucharistic celebration. They take Communion to the elderly, give friends a ride to church, cook countless meals, and quietly give hours and hours to soup kitchens and food pantries. They devote much time and energy behind the scenes. Sometimes one will even donate a new sound system so that even the hard of hearing can make out the words of the homily.

Too often we overlook the quiet people in our lives. Parents, teachers, pastors, friends, and many others whose names we may not even know give of themselves in inconspicuous ways because the love of Christ empowers them. We should all make an effort to look carefully in out-of-the-way places to spot and acknowledge those who serve and yet draw no attention to themselves. It is with grateful hearts that we thank God for the "possums" in our churches and in our lives.

Slipcovers

Our parents liked to cover things up. Perhaps the fear that anything of value might be destroyed followed them out of the Great Depression. Women wore aprons in the kitchen. Hallway carpets had "runners" to keep the center from showing wear. The dining-room table was protected by a table pad, over which Grandma spread a linen cloth, which in turn was covered with a plastic protector…except on Sundays. Remember doilies? We still have a drawer full of those little circles that Grandma crocheted to protect the arm rests of every chair. We also have some of those long, hand-embroidered "dresser scarves" she used to keep the bedroom furniture from getting scratched. Every well-dressed sofa had a slipcover or at least a "throw" that could be whisked away if company knocked at the door.

As for actually using anything good—that could be downright sinful. The china and silver might show up on the adult table at Thanksgiving, Christmas, and Easter. Beyond that, it seemed satisfaction enough for our parents to know that they had fine things locked up until an important person or occasion turned up. They believed that with proper care, beautiful things would last forever. The main goal was to leave everything of value in perfect condition and pass it on to the next generation. Of course, not having used any of these things as children, the next generation often felt little connection to them. When Grandma passed away, the chair she sat in for many years remained spotless, but the springs inside were broken. We still have her china to pass on to the children. The doilies and dresser scarves are so out of style that some heir will likely dispose of them at a yard sale.

We should all take stock of what we are keeping locked away. What are we saving for some distant day of celebration? Have we locked away forgiveness for a friend until the day he or she repents? Are we withholding love from a parent or child who disappointed us? What gifts and talents do we keep covered because of fear to use them? Sometimes we keep our real treasures stored away so safely that they never get any use at all.

The wine Jesus provided for the wedding at Cana offered an abundance of the best. Maybe it is time to make every day a celebration by pouring out the best in our hearts and our homes. A news item reported that immediately following September 11, 2001, restaurant owners noted a marked increase in the number of people ordering dessert. Did we finally understand how brief life is? In making everyday use of our best, we accomplish two things: Our loved ones know how much we treasure them and we make memories that bind our hearts together.

Spare Change

When pennies, nickels, dimes, and quarters spilled over the top of the pickle jar and onto our dresser, the time had come to count the contents of our spare change jar. Within an hour, we had a stack of neatly rolled coins on the kitchen table. The total amount of fifty-five dollars amazed us.

Spare change had a special place in the houses in which we grew up. Grandpa Cavera collected his in a certain drawer. Sometimes he gave a grandchild the job of counting the coins. Afterward, the child received a gift of the counted money. Grandpa Smith kept a ten-gallon jug behind his bedroom door, a fitting tribute to his ever-optimistic outlook. Our modest quart jar fills quickly, which may say something about our own generation's need to see immediate results.

Somewhere between our generation and the one coming after us, there has been a fundamental shift in the way we think about spare change. "Spare" once meant something extra that had value and should be saved for a time of need. We had spare tires and blankets and even a spare room. As children, we understood two-cent pop bottles might be collected and exchanged for a few coins to provide an afternoon at a Saturday matinee with Flash Gordon.

Now, change is considered "loose" rather than "spare." Loose change is useful only when left as a tip for poor service. It falls between sofa cushions and rolls beneath vending machines. Hidden in dark corners, loose change remains forever worthless. Loose change and loose people lack focus. Consequently neither ever seems to amount to much.

Sometimes the difference between spare change and loose coins is relative. In the Gospel of Mark (12:41–44), the widow with no change to spare offered her last two coins, and they became more than enough. On the other hand, the rich offered large sums that meant nothing more to them than loose change.

Perhaps change jars began disappearing when we lost the ability to see that the sum total of life is made up of smaller bits and pieces. We have forgotten that acts of kindness or moments of joy eventually make up the sum of who we become. For the most part, we have become a loose people, throwing away minutes on worthless passions instead of cherishing and spending wisely the seemingly small, spare moments of the journey of life. Have we forgotten that both spare change and spare time can add up to a surprising sum?

Time Travel

In Revelation 21:5, we are reminded that God said, "See, I am making all things new." Recently, that verse resonated with us through several events in our lives. A group of Tibetan monks came to town for the week. Before one of our weekday masses, they graced us with a chant. Their deep tones blended human voices in patterns unfamiliar to our ears. Their song resonated with the majesty of mountain peaks and deep valleys, of water rushing over rocks and cliffs in a country far away. The voices of the monks took us to their home. We wondered what they would think if we gave them a sample of who we are through our music.

For us, the end of the week continued to flow from Tibet back into time. It had been fifty years since either of us had sat in the back seat of a '51 Chevy. As soon as we climbed into our friends' car, memories came back. The ceiling inside was higher than in today's cars. Of course, men wore hats back then. Our friend reminisced about playing with toys on the floorboard in the back seat and even taking naps on the ample shelf under the rear window. This car had no seatbelts, radio, or air conditioner.

We cruised town with the windows down and air blowing through our hair.

After a leisurely supper, we parked near the levee down by the river. A breeze blew off the water, and the sky had turned orange and gold. Families with babies in strollers, people on bicycles, and couples holding hands were all there for no reason other than the simple pleasure of walking with no place to go. For the final event of the evening, we sat outdoors at an ice-cream shop where, lick by lick, we savored cones. So much of this reminded us of our childhood when "going out" meant watching sunsets by the water, feeding bread to ducks, or sitting on a porch swing and talking.

We thought about all of this while we took our walk this morning. We always finish our walk by climbing a hill near our house. This is probably the most aerobic thing either of us does all week. As we neared the top, a neighbor who is retired came striding downhill in the opposite direction. "It's easier going this way," he said. Jim muttered, "Everything's' easier for him. He's retired." We found ourselves wondering how it is that at our age we still find ourselves "climbing hills."

Monks who carry their home in their voices, the grace of a well-aged car, the magnificence of a river sunset, a cone savored at an outside table, and the strength to still climb uphill make us thankful for all that is. It is by learning to "be" rather than to always "do" and by welcoming what grace brings into our lives that we are able to see how God, at every moment, is making all things new.